THE RENAISSANCE RECONSIDERED

A SYMPOSIVM

LEONA GABEL

RUTH L. KENNEDY

RUTH W. KENNEDY

GUNTER LEWY

SIDNEY R. PACKARD

MAX SALVADORI

1964
VOLUME XLIV
SMITH COLLEGE STUDIES IN HISTORY
NORTHAMPTON · MASSACHUSETTS

PREFACE

"Es ist eine alte Geschichte
Doch bleibt sie ewig neu"
Heine

With the present volume, the forty-fourth in the series, the Smith College Studies in History are celebrating their own minor rebirth. The last publication to appear, six years ago, was the translation of the last four books of *The Commentaries of Pius II* by Florence Gragg and Leona C. Gabel.

Miss Gabel has long been associated with these studies. Her first contribution was published in 1928-29 and between 1937 and 1957 appeared *The Commentaries* for which she provided the Introduction and the historical notes. From 1951-1957 she also served on the editorial board. It seemed therefore eminently fitting that a revival of the studies should occur with a volume of essays which grew out of a symposium occasioned by her retirement in 1963. Four of the papers were actually delivered at the symposium The Renaissance Reconsidered (April 1963), two of them were contributed by colleagues of Miss Gabel. They are connected not only as reappraisals of that most controversial of epochs, but as offerings to a medievalist who became a Renaissance scholar.

When Jacob Burckhardt published *Die Kultur der Renaissance in Italien* roughly a hundred years ago, he provided work for scholars for generations to come. Twenty years ago Lynn Thorndike exclaimed "What is the use of questioning the Renaissance? No one has ever proved its existence; no one has really tried to."[1] And yet, as long as historians will concern themselves with time, with ends and with beginnings, as long as we will take pleasure in the luminous colors of Botticelli's paintings, as long as we will view with wonder the buildings of fifteenth and sixteenth century Rome, there will be reappraisals of that era, which has its roots firmly anchored in the medieval world, and the end of which may be in 1559 in Italy but perhaps not until the seventeenth century in Spain.

In the present volume a medievalist will look at the Renaissance; two Renaissance scholars, an historian and an art historian will examine (as they did so many times in the past in a joint seminar) different aspects of the first revival of Rome; a modern historian will scrutinize the end of the Renaissance in Italy; a political theorist will illuminate some particular facets of disquisitions on tyranny and a critic of Spanish literature will discuss a satire of the late Spanish Renaissance. All separate little beads, but strung on the thread of a common interest. An old story perhaps, but eternally new in the unfinished debate of history.

Nelly S. Hoyt

[1] "Renaissance or Prenaissance" *Journal of The History of Ideas*, 1943, p. 74.

TABLE OF CONTENTS

SMITH COLLEGE STUDIES IN HISTORY

Nelly S. Hoyt

Nina Garsoian   Allan Mitchell

Editors

The SMITH COLLEGE STUDIES IN HISTORY, begun in 1915 under the editorship of Sidney B. Fay, has published to date something over sixty books and monographs in various fields of history. The range of subjects has been intentionally wide, including the fields of American and European history, and stretching in time from the Ancient world to the present. The STUDIES has published monographic research as well as critical editions in translation of significant historical documents.

It is the aim of the STUDIES to afford a medium for the publication of works and monographs in history by present and former members of the Smith College faculty and graduate students. Correspondence concerning contributions should be addressed to Nelly S. Hoyt. Orders for copies or requests for exchange should be addressed to the Smith College Library.

A MEDIEVALIST LOOKS AT THE RENAISSANCE.[1]

Sidney R. Packard

Professor Emeritus of History, Smith College.

A distinguished English medievalist, Norman H. Baynes, once began his remarks, made under somewhat similar circumstances, with a statement which will at least serve as an adequate warning to this audience. "If the mouths of the academically dead are doomed to an unbroken silence, the tongue of the academically retired but still functioning may perhaps be permitted to wag in a garrulity which recognizes the now or neverness of its opportunity."[2] Thus I shall not limit myself to the brief statement that any medievalist who looks at the Renaissance is sure to take a very dim view of the whole matter, despite the reluctant necessity of admitting, in the end, that there was something there and that it needs a name.

Moreover, and this is an additional risk for you, I am not going to talk primarily of any medievalist looking at the Renaissance, but of this one. You are in for some reminiscence whether you will or no.

It was by pure chance a half-century ago that I, as a sophomore seven miles across the river from here, at an institution of which you may have heard,[3] had a free elective and inserted in my program of study, for my own pleasure, a course in history. The course was that old perennial, Europe from the Fall of Rome to 1648 (whether modern practice to thin this out and get it down to 1963 is a better or a worse procedure is, as the phrase goes, another question).

In this course we read Edward Gibbon's *Decline and Fall of the Roman Empire* (1776-1788) and the *Renaissance in Italy* (1875-1886) by J. A. Symonds, the latter a rather neurotic literary person thoroughly saturated with the ideas of Jacob Burckhardt as contained in his essay entitled *The Civilization of the Renaissance in Italy* (1860).[4] As a result we were completely convinced that the Middle Ages were a thousand years of unredeemed gloom and darkness, suddenly, miraculously, and providentially illuminated at long last by that flash of blinding light which was Italy in the fourteenth and fifteenth centuries, i.e., The Renaissance with a capital R, à la Jacob Burck-

[1] In preparing this paper for publication the author has been uncomfortably aware of the fact that it was meant to serve as an introduction to a symposium in honor of a colleague and was designed for presentation to a specific audience and not for publication at all. This will explain and, hopefully, justify a pervading personal note. The paper also contains several allusions more meaningful on this campus than elsewhere: readers from elsewhere will derive some help in each instance from the foot-notes.

[2] *Byzantine Studies and Other Essays* (London: 1955), 272-273.

[3] Amherst College.

[4] Published originally as *Die Kultur der Renaissance in Italien* (Basel: 1860).

hardt. This was, in the earlier classic phrase of Michelet, "The Discovery of the World and of Man".

This happy state of affairs, according to Burckhardt and his followers, could only have come about in Italy and only in the fourteenth and fifteenth centuries, steeped as Italy then was and had long been in the hectic political, economic, and predominantly secular activities of the Italian city-states. An additional and essential factor was the intellectual and cultural invigoration that came at that time and in that place from a new awareness of the secular nature and accomplishments of pre-Christian Greece and Rome. All this produced a new ferment of mind and spirit and released the enormous but hitherto latent energies which led on to Michelangelo and his fellows. The Renaissance, so defined, spread rather slowly and fitfully but inexorably across the Alps and eventually into the uttermost limits of Europe, rather like a bit of quicksilver, and thus produced the modern world. So ran the theory, still to be found in many of our books, though not now in quite such an exaggerated form.

As a graduate student at Harvard, with a naïveté which now seems to me absolutely incredible, I came only slowly to the realization that the Burckhardt theory, no matter how engagingly presented by Symonds and others, was hardly completely sound. In a course which it was my good fortune to have under Professor Ephraim Emerton, on the Renaissance and the Reformation, there was additional enlightenment. Emerton, as genial as he was learned, remarked to the class one day in his usual quiet manner, but with a twinkle in his eye, that Burckhardt seems to have thought that the Turks captured Constantinople on a fine day in May in 1453 (which they did) and that all the Greek scholars then resident in the city took the night express and started the Renaissance in Florence the following morning. Yet even Emerton would not concede real individualism to Innocent III, to St. Bernard, or even to Abelard.

When I came to Smith, and I assure you that this was after and not before the Biblical Flood, actually in 1921, I was still thinking and when necessary lecturing, with illustrations, on the Renaissance as the Discovery of the World and of Man, with all its implications, although I was beginning to insert some very serious doubts and modifications, particularly time-wise. The result was that in the sections of History 11 which fell to my lot in the later twenties and for many years thereafter (how we teachers do cling to the 'gimmicks' that seem to work!) there was a quite proper discussion of the Renaissance based on the reading assigned but, as the hour progressed, we indulged more and more in revolutionary reflections on the dates involved, thereby pushing back the beginning of the movement to 1250 or even much earlier. This led inevitably to a discussion of the Renaissance elements to be seen so clearly in the Middle Ages and elsewhere than in Italy and was followed by some examination of the medieval elements so evident in the Renaissance in Italy even in the fifteenth century. This was all meant to work up to a kind of climactic question "Was there a Renaissance at all?" asked by the instructor just as the bell rang, thus precluding any answer. It worked very well and left the class in that frame of mind saturated with doubt leading on to inquiry which Abelard identified long ago as the best road to wisdom and learning. I never got a response but once. It came from a student in the front row, a very satisfactory student whom I shall not, of course, identify, though perhaps you are entitled to a slight hint in order to appreciate the episode properly (her mother gave the Engel lecture here last November).[5] Her shout "If there was no Renaissance, what would become of my family?" came forth with irresistible spontaneity in the split-second following the question. My students have often left me speechless but never before or since on quite so memorable an occasion.

There were other experiences of disillusionment with the old Michelet-Burckhardt formula though I will spare you most of the detail. I remember a dinner of the Medieval Academy of America, for example, probably in the middle thirties, when the after-dinner speakers, with no Renaissance experts present, devoted themselves to the nature and the importance of the 'so-called Renaissance'. They had themselves a veritable field-day.

In the mid-twenties, and for some eighteen years thereafter, I taught a course here in early modern French history, with a suitable and of course an extensive medieval introduction, and quickly discovered that there were many evidences of a Renaissance in France long before 1494 and that the transmission of the Italian Renaissance to France via the expedition of Charles VIII into Italy in 1494 was an absurd idea anyhow, no matter how persuasively or how frequently presented. A military expedition, and especially that one, as a channel for the transmission of cultural ideas, *quelle idée!* (Yet a book has just been announced, with 235 illustrations, on *The France of the Renaissance, 1488-1559!*[6])

Then I taught for some twenty-five years or so a course in medieval English history and found many of the usual Renaissance characteristics even there, long before the arrival of Erasmus and his associates.

Finally, as many of you know, some of you perhaps to your sorrow, I have been attempting to teach the cultural and intellectual history of the Middle Ages for a good many years, including this one. No man who has done this can ever believe that humanism, individualism, the discovery of the world and of man, secularism, or even conscious pride in achievement, or whatever else has come to be traditionally the characteristic features of the Renaissance with a capital R, came as late as the fourteenth and fifteenth

---

[5] Many members of the audience knew that the Engel lecture in the preceding November was actually given by the fourth speaker at this symposium. She and her husband are both Professors Emeriti of Art at Smith College and both are well-known specialists in the field of Renaissance art.

[6] A. Daneuil (Paris: 1962).

centuries and only in Italy. John of Salisbury, Gerald of Wales, Abelard and Heloise,[7] Alain de Lille, Bernard of Morlaix, to mention no others, all living in the twelfth century, practically destroy the Burckhardtian view. And the quicksilver theory of its spread from any central point, Italy or elsewhere, is at least as absurd as the simile suggests.

After all, the practising medievalist has already experienced the Carolingian Renaissance, the Ottonian Renaissance, and the Renaissance of the Twelfth Century before he ever reaches the Renaissance with a capital R. Professor Lopez, moreover, even thinks he has found a Renaissance in that most unlikely of all places, the tenth century.[8] Renaissances in the plural do seem to kill off any concept of *the* Renaissance in the singular, limited to a particular time and place.

Because of all this, I made a standing offer long ago to my colleague, Miss Gabel, who has given our course on the Renaissance for many years, to lecture in her course at any time on the essential fallacy involved in the usual concept of the Renaissance. She never accepted my generous offer though she was much too polite to counter with a suggestion that she might lecture to my students doing the same thing for the usual stereotype of the Middle Ages, a period which has certainly been quite as badly misread over the years and still is in some quarters.

We have, as I suppose and hope you all know, both change and continuity in history. The change is never sudden or complete and the continuity, though partial, is equally fundamental. Our periodization, therefore, the Middle Ages, the Renaissance, the Reformation, the Enlightenment, etc., are only terms or labels contsructed for our own convenience. They are not discrete entities which start and stop at fixed moments and they cannot be characterized completely and finally by any definition. If we have in fact sold our souls to these labels of our own making it is certainly entirely our own fault.

Professor Douglas Bush, in a little book entitled *The Renaissance and English Humanism,* has brought out in a rather striking way the perils that lurk in definitions. The quest for a satisfactory formula for the Ranaissance, he says, is doomed from the start.[9]

> Imagine an historian of A.D. 2500 trying to define the civilization of the United States in the early 20th century in the light of its literature. He will see that it was an age of realistic revolt and he will summon a cloud of witnesses: Theodore Dreiser, H. L. Mencken, Sinclair Lewis, Edgar Lee Masters, Eugene O'Neill, John Dos Passos, Ernest Hemingway, Robinson Jeffers, William Faulkner, Erskine Caldwell, and James T. Farrell. The obvious verdict will be that the United States was

[7] See E. Gilson, *Heloise and Abelard* (Chicago: 1951), *passim,* but especially chapter viii, for a remarkable presentation of this assertion.
[8] R. S. Lopez, "Still Another Renaissance?", *American Historical Review,* LVII: 1951, 1-21.
[9] Douglas Bush, *The Renaissance and English Humanism* (London: 1939), 16-17.

populated by commercial brigands, fundamentalists, blind reactionaries, drunkards, wastrels, hypocrites, fools, knaves, gunmen and perverts, and that no ray of intelligence, virtue, culture, or idealism could pierce the darkness. - - - - But another historian with another set of preconceptions might survey the same field. The typical voice of Vachel Lindsay will assure him that the American soul was in tune with the Y.M.C.A. Robert Frost will show him the homely goodwill and integrity of rural life. Willa Cather will celebrate pioneer courage and traditional faith. And the south of Ellen Glasgow will be the home, not of degraded besiality, but of highly civilized conversation and behaviour. Philosophic moralists such as Irving Babbitt and Paul Elmer More will make a stern appeal to order and authority. Yet these completely different pictures can be made out of the literature of one country over one short period. What of the civilizations of half a dozen countries over several hundred years?

This is not the place or the time for a complete, definitive, and critical estimate of the Renaissance as of now. A professor, after all, is probably only a sort of foghorn that indicates the fog but does nothing to disperse it, as Douglas Bush himself suggests on another page in the same book. We can and we should grant high praise to Burckhardt's book which even he called only an essay. It opened up new approaches to historical studies and has been influential in transforming the western attitude toward the past. As Denis Hay has recently pointed out,[10] Burckhardt may have neglected economic facts (many to be sure not available to him anyhow), his chronology is biased, he has ignored northern Europe too much, he thought the study of the antique in art beneficial but the same study in letters stifling, he claimed too much, far too much we now know, for Renaissance science, and he claimed too much both for Italian virtues and perhaps even for Italian vices. Much of this can be forgiven a man writing in 1860, though perhaps not his virtual equation of the modern world with fifteenth century Italy. But when we all try to get at the spirit of an age through every possible channel, including art and morals, etc., we are following to a considerable extent a path marked out very plainly by Jacob Burckhardt.

It will suffice perhaps merely to say, but with great emphasis, that the term Renaissance is now no longer sacrosanct either as to chronology, locale, character, content, scope, or transmission.

The evidence (except for art and vernacular literature) for putting the Renaissance in the twelfth century was attractively presented in a major volume by Professor Haskins in 1927 (I well remember the gleam in his eye when he told me what the title was to be). He did not, of course, create the term 'twelfth century Renaissance': it had been used earlier by another great American medievalist, Dana C. Munro, but only for a short paper.[11]

---

[10] "Burckhardt's 'Renaissance': 1860-1960" in *History Today* (January, 1960), 4 ff.
[11] "Renaissance of the Twelfth Century" in *American Historical Association, Annual Report for 1906* (Washington: 1908), I, 43-49.

That title, in 1927, for a serious work by a first-rate scholar, was something of a bombshell and was quite obviously meant to be just that. The influence of the book was and has been continuously enormous: as it has been said, everybody has at least read the title.

I can cite a long list of competent scholars on both sides of the Atlantic who will now put the Renaissance in the twelfth century and I can cite a large number of interesting and varied definitions of the Renaissance occasioned or at least supported by the material assembled in this book. The literature of the subject, however, has become by now so extensive that I shall, by necessity, limit myself to a relatively few examples.

Maritain sees the scholastics as the first humanists[12] and Gilson thinks the dissemination of Aristotle in the twelfth and thirteenth centuries did more to spread antique ideas than the later construction of imitation verses à la Homer[13]. E. H. Harbison, from the viewpoint of the intellectual historian, feels that the most exciting half-century since the fall of Rome is the first half of the twelfth century.[14] George Sarton thinks that the twelfth century constituted a real Renaissance.[15] Lynn White, in two remarkable articles, recently in *Speculum*[16] and in the *American Historical Review*,[17] has come close to demonstrating effectively that modern science stems in fact from the twelfth century, including but not limited to technology.

A Swedish scholar, Johan Nordström, in his *Moyen Age et Renaissance*, published in the French translation in 1933,[18] has gone the whole way, characterizing the Italian Renaissance as only a moment in a general European movement, not a revolution or even a renovation, but merely a flowery branch of a powerful tree, namely the Middle Ages. Since I seem to possess the only copy of this book in Northampton (I picked it up quite by chance in 1935 at a stall in the *Place du Théâtre Français* in Paris), I will indicate its content in somewhat more detail.

Nordström makes the whole Renaissance movement fundamentally twelfth century, north European, and specifically French. He stresses the growing secularism resulting from the crusades, expanding commerce and the rise of towns, cites the career of Abelard and the introduction of Greek science via Arabic Spain in the twelfth century as a crucial chapter in intellectual history,

---

[12] J. Maritain, *True Humanism* (New York: 1938), p. xv and chapter i, *passim*.
[13] E. Gilson, "Humanisme médiéval et Renaissance" in his *Les idées et les lettres* (Paris: 1938).
[14] *The Christian Scholar and the Age of the Reformation* (New York: 1956), 19.
[15] *Introduction to the History of Science*, II (Washington: 1931) 2. Sarton feels that the Renaissance was not a renaissance in science and that the humanists were anti-scientific in their thinking: see his "Science and the Renaissance" in *The Civilization of the Renaissance* (Chicago: 1929), 75-98.
[16] "Technology and Invention in the Middle Ages", *Speculum*, XV: 1940, 141-159: this is also available in an expanded form in his *Medieval Technology and Social Change* (Oxford: 1962) 1-177 (with illustrations).
[17] "Naturalistic Science and Naturalistic Art", *American Historical Review*, LII: 1947, 421-435.
[18] The original Swedish edition was published in 1929.

and indicates the presence of the love element in much twelfth century poetry, notably in the *Carmina Burana.* He even finds the love of nature in some monastic circles. He sees realism in French twelfth century art, thinks even Petrarch was mostly French, asserts that Boccaccio was born in Paris, insists that the *Decameron* depends upon the medieval *fabliau,* and claims that the Renard the Fox story displays classical influences even in its earlier versions. He is particularly ingenious in his study of southern France and especially of Provence, insisting upon many and powerful influences flowing in this period from France into Italy, later dramatically personified in St. Francis. He certainly makes all the streams run in his direction. His conclusion is that Italy was a cultural province of France in the twelfth century and following, and that this explains both the origin and the nature of the much less important, later movement known as the Italian Renaissance.

Erwin Panofsky, in a recent work entitled *Renaissance and Renascences in Western Art,*[19] has made a notable contribution to the literature concerned with the origin and nature of the Renaissance, based on an elaborate and masterly study of the art involved. (He says that some of his statements will be understood only by art historians and this I am willing to concede.) He finds more than one proto-renaissance in the twelfth century even in art and has the illustrations to prove his point, but he insists that there was nonetheless a real Renaissance in Italy in the fifteenth century. The medieval idea of antiquity, he thinks, was concrete, incomplete, and distorted: the Italian Renaissance view of antiquity was comprehensive, consistent, and abstract. He notes the importance of the time element: the Middle Ages were too near to antiquity and tried, not with great success, to hold on to parts of it, whereas the Italian Renaissance was far enough away from antiquity, though surrounded by its ruins, to see it as a whole and to understand its essence.

The variety of comments by scholars who look upon the Renaissance as a movement quite different from the older concept is considerable. Carl Stephenson thought the term "meaningless except to describe Italian art in the fifteenth century".[20] G. C. Sellery has insisted that the Renaissance was "all a matter of human energy: the phenomena constituted the Renaissance and were not caused by it".[21] G. R. Elton feels that the term Renaissance, except perhaps in the arts, represents only an abstraction of the historian which he now labors to destroy.[22] J. Godard calls it not a unified movement but a chronological ensemble of different and largely unrelated facts.[23] Myron Gilmore has asserted that the term has blocked proper interpretation more

[19] (Copenhagen: 1960) in two volumes.
[20] *Medieval History* (New York: 1935), 709-720, especially 720.
[21] *The Renaissance, Its Nature and Origins* (Madison: 1950), especially 257 ff.
[22] *English Historical Review,* LXVIII: 1953, 277.
[23] *Revue historique,* CCXI: 1954, 114-115.

than it has helped.[24] Arnold Toynbee calls the term unscientific, insidious, and subjective.[25]. J. D. Mackie is more positive in his criticism and maintains that the Renaissance was not an event but a process, the revolt of the facts as against the theories in church, state, morality, philosophy, economics, etc.[26]

The most devastating criticism of the Renaissance concept may actually come from Herbert Butterfield in a paper which should be more widely known, "History of Science and the Study of History" in the *Harvard Library Bulletin* for 1959. He there asserts that the history of science, not of sciences, changes the whole schematization of traditional European history. On this basis, both the Renaissance and the Reformation fade from view as vital concepts. To Oriental scholars, for example, Renaissance and Reformation are meaningless terms. The scientific revolution of the seventeenth century, on the other hand, is a vital concept of the first importance for everybody. The seventeenth century scientific revolution produced our modern world: compared with it the Renaissance, however defined, has only a very limited kind of originality.

One of the most interesting reactions to the older views of the Renaissance comes from the pages of one of the most distinguished of all the medievalists produced on this side of the Atlantic. Henry Osborn Taylor prided himself that he wrote two volumes on *Thought and Expression in the Sixteenth Century*[27] and never once mentioned the Renaissance. In his two earlier volumes on *The Mediaeval Mind,* first published in 1911,[28] the word appears only once in the index and the reference is to a note on the misleading nature of the term. In this note[29] he also suggests that we should get rid of all renaissances, Carolingian, Ottonian, and Italian and substitute a concept of history stressing continuity. The term, he says (and those of us who had the privilege of knowing him can almost hear him saying it), "carries more false notions than can be corrected on a summer's day". Each century, including the sixteenth, he thought, draws on the past and produces much not exclusively its own.[30] There can be a new tone and a new temper but even these will be powerfully influenced by prior expressions, whether in language, stone, or in other media. The glory of the sixteenth century, he insists,[31] is in new and abler forms of expression, not in new content or in

[24] M. P. Gilmore, *The World of Humanism,* 1453-1517 (New York: 1952), p. xiii.
[25] *A Study of History,* IX (London: 1954), 1.
[26] *The Earlier Tudors, 1485-1558* (Oxford: 1952), 1.
[27] (New York: 1920).
[28] (London and New York: 1911), two volumes.
[29] I, 211, n. 2.
[30] Cf. his "Placing the Middle Ages" in *Harvard Tercentenary Publications; Independence, Convergence, and Borrowings* (Cambridge: 1937) 151-166 (also in *Speculum,* XI: 437-445) for a persuasive statement of the same idea in relation to the Middle Ages.
[31] *Thought and Expression in the Sixteenth Century,* II, 373-387, especially 373-374 and 383.

new emotional factors. V. L. Saulnier, in his preface[32] to the French translation in 1950 of *The Renaissance in Historical Thought* by Wallace K.
Ferguson, would seem to agree: the Renaissance, he says, was not a transition but a period of *chef-d'oeuvres* which completed earlier developments.

The mandatory conclusion to all this is some indication as to where I
stand in relation to the various concepts of the Renaissance, old and new.
(I am reminded of a visit to the big Mo, in naval parlance the battle-wagon
Missouri, after the war, when my young Ensign host explained to me very
carefully just where General MacArthur stood and just where the Japanese
envoys stood when the surrender terms were signed and then, with equal
seriousness, explained just where *he* stood at that historic moment.)

I think I stand with Wallace Ferguson, not mainly I hope because of that
notable chapter on The Revolt of the Medievalists in his major work, but
because he has emphasized in all his writings that the Renaissance was an
era of transition from the medieval to the modern, a fundamental change in
Europe from a world essentially ecclesiastical, feudal, and agricultural to one
that was urban, secular, and national (with a very small n). This change, he
thinks, was inevitably reflected in art and in literature, in a larger population, in relative peace and order and in longer and more fruitful application
of human skills and energies. There was also a revival of the antique, but
this is as likely the result as the cause of these changes and is in any event
a relatively minor aspect of the whole complex which we should recognize
as the Renaissance.[33]

The term Renaissance is obviously a necessary tool in historical instruc-
tion, comparable with such other terms as Middle Ages, Modern World, East
and West, etc. These tags have great usefulness but they are dangerous
snares for the unwary. The Renaissance is real but not so sudden or as bright
as it has been painted, just as the Middle Ages are certainly less dark and less
static than they have been pictured.[34] There was a Renaissance in the twelfth
century and there was a Renaissance in Italy in the fourteenth and fifteenth
centuries and the existence of each modifies fundamentally our views of both.

The medievalist in these parts who has taken the longest look at the
Renaissance is certainly Leona Christine Gabel. She was trained originally
as a medievalist at Bryn Mawr under a great master, Howard L. Gray, and

---

[32] J. Marty, *La renaissance dans la pensée historique* (Paris: 1950), p. xv.

[33] Ferguson's ideas are to be found briefly stated in his *The Renaissance* (New York:
1940) in the *Berkshire Studies in European History* and more at length in his *The
Renaissance in Historical Thought: Five Centuries of Interpretation* (Boston: 1948)
and in many articles and papers in various publications. See especially his "The Interpretation of the Renaissance: Suggestions for a Synthesis," *Journal of the History of
Ideas,* XII: 1951, 483-495 and his "The Reinterpretation of the Renaissance" in *Facets
of the Renaissance* (Los Angeles: 1959), 1-18.

[34] C. H. Haskins, *The Renaissance of the Twelfth Century* (Cambridge: 1927),
p. vii.

her first published work was in the medieval field,[35] although her teaching and her considerable publications over the last four decades have been in the Renaissance.

Probably no period in history should ever be taught by a teacher who knows only that field. Beware of the modern historian whose knowledge starts in 1870 or, worse, in 1918. Of course we cannot all go so far as the distinguished colleague who is about to follow me on this platform.[36] Not only is he thoroughly at home as a human being in three major countries but as a scholar, if one can make such a distinction, he is unusually competent not only in his special field of modern European history but also in the ancient field and, to a very considerable extent, in all the periods in between.

If I may be permitted to say so (and I do not know who has a better right after my forty years of academic cooperative activity both pedagogical and administrative with the lady in question) the field of the Renaissance in our History department has not only been in exceptionally capable hands during these four decades but, from the viewpoint of this medievalist, in safe hands.[37] I can only join you in the hope that the field will be as well cultivated in the next forty years, and as safely.

---

[35] L. C. Gabel, *Benefit of Clergy in England in the Later Middle Ages* (Northampton: 1929) in *Smith Studies in History,* XIV, Nos. 1-4.

[36] Professor Max Salvadori.

[37] The course in question has always been entitled The Age of Renaissance and the Reformation, with a subtitle, A Study of the Transition from Medieval to Modern Times. I know that the word "modern" has bothered Miss Gabel a good deal, but no medievalist can possibly object to this title.

THE FIRST REVIVAL OF ROME 1420 - 1484

Professor Emeritus of History,

Smith College

One statement which can safely be made about the Renaissance is that it is in a chronic state of being reconsidered. As is well known, the concept of a revival, rebirth, "Renaissance" in fifteenth and sixteenth century Italy is a legacy from the so-called Renaissance itself, conveying not only a judgment concerning that epoch but actually creating the pattern of periodization — ancient, medieval, modern — which has bedevilled historiography ever since. It is now generally conceded that the Renaissance was not a rebirth of classical arts and letters in quite the sense maintained by the Italian humanists of that day; yet this negative conclusion does not dispose of the fact that the idea of recovery was in the air, whether as a goal eagerly awaited or later as a proud achievement. Nor was it limited to the cultural realm. In the welter of conflicting interpretations of the epoch, this consciousness of revival, of beginning afresh, remains a significant fact supporting the view of the Renaissance as an identifiable period and movement in European history.

It is our purpose on this occasion to examine a single though highly significant facet of Italian history in the fifteenth century — the first revival of Rome and the papacy. Viewed in its larger context, the subject illustrates the variety of forces contributing to a sense of renewal or restoration, forces for which the renewed vogue of classical antiquity supplied a congenial focus or symbol. It has the special merit of exhibiting an unmistakably medieval institution and its fate in a critical era of transition.

For an era of crisis it assuredly was. Europe was in the throes of what has been called the "century of catastrophes" extending roughly from about 1330 to the second half of the fifteenth century and punctuated with major disasters both natural and man-made. It was a period of incessant and devastating wars, of frequent crop failures and famine, of recurrent epidemics. The Black Death alone left a death-toll outstripping that of war and famine put together. In the wake of these disasters came an economic depression of major proportions rendered acute by the closing of eastern trade markets. The depression struck town and country alike, though not necessarily at the same time or in the same degree in the various countries of Europe. Social unrest was widespread. A way out of this dismal state of affairs was not only eagerly awaited throughout European society but a goal consciously pursued by Church councils and parliaments, by feudal lord and peasant, by clerics and laity. Would salvation lie in the restoration of an older order or follow new paths? Would its course be gradual or convulsive?

For the papacy this turbulent epoch was marked by more than seventy years of exile from Rome — willing exile, for the most part — in southern France and Avignon (1305-1378); forty years more of schism (1378-1417) which saw at first two, then three popes simultaneously claiming the headship of Christendom. Exile lent it a French rather than a universal character in the eyes of European Christendom; schism destroyed its unity. Together they reduced it to a pawn in the major political wars which were rending Europe. When the fifteenth century opened, the papacy had virtually lost control of the States of the Church; its spiritual leadership in Western Christendom was bankrupt. A burgeoning demand for reform of the Church in head and members was already expressing itself in a succession of ecumenical councils which gravely threatened the authority of the pope.

Thus when Martin V, a Roman and a Colonna, was elected pope in 1417 at the Council of Constance in token of a reunited Christendom centered eventually in the Eternal City, a very special set of problems confronted him and would continue to plague his successors. To begin with, the Council of Constance to which he owed his election had in the interests of unity and reform proclaimed the supremacy of conciliar authority in the Church and the right of a Council to depose popes if necessary. Thus armed, it had enjoined upon Martin a program of reforms. The papal treasury furthermore was seriously depleted. Meanwhile Rome and the States of the Church were in the hands of local barons and powerful mercenaries; it took Martin two years even to gain entry into the city. Rome itself was a no-man's land, its populace a rabble, its churches and civic buildings in ruins, its economic life at a standstill; a "city of cowards" it was termed, in which the fierce feuds of rival nobility were the order — or disorder — of the day. Papal prestige here as elsewhere in Europe was at an all-time low. And all the while there loomed ever more threateningly on the eastern horizon the Turkish invasion. These were the problems confronting Martin V and his successors for years to come. The revival of Rome, however envisaged by individual popes, had to take account of these stern realities.

Whether from necessity or choice or both, the task given priority by the popes was the recovery of Rome and the Patrimony of the Church. The States of the Church had since the early Middle Ages been a major concern of the papacy. Now their recovery was a task which had to be done over and over again, and involved the popes in wars not only with local usurpers but with other states of Italy. As success gradually crowned their efforts it was but a short step from the reconquest of lost territories to an outright policy of expansion — by purchase, by nepotism or by naked force. Thus the restoration of the States of the Church took on peninsular dimensions from the very outset and soon penetrated the arena of European power politics.

This was not in itself a new experience in the history of the papacy; its novelty lay in the changed circumstances which shaped the course of papal policy and transformed its character and goals. A few illustrations will suffice.

That Martin V should desire to return to Rome and to restore the Papal States was natural enough. He was a Roman and a member of one of its oldest and most powerful families. The financial straits of the papacy, whose income is estimated to have been reduced to a third of its former amount, lent the further incentive of recovering the revenues of the Patrimony. In the circumstances the only means available to Martin for dealing with the powerful condottieri and local feudatories then in control of papal lands was to send other mercenaries against them or to purchase the doubtful loyalty of usurpers who could not otherwise be dislodged. A Colonna himself, Martin freely enlisted the services of his own ambitious Colonna relatives. And since the wages of this gentry far outran the resources of the papal treasury, it became customary to assign to them for a specified term the revenues from individual towns or to bestow vicariates upon them outright. The title of papal vicar might thus mean nothing more than a token recognition by its incumbent of papal overlordship. Yet such concessions on the part of this shrewd Pontiff should not be construed as weakness. On the contrary, what he yielded for the time being in direct political control was turned to immediate financial advantage by attaching substantial fees to such appointments. For the title of papal vicar did confer a kind of legal status upon these local tyrants which they on the whole found worth the price. Although Martin unquestionably gave to Rome its first taste of order and prosperity in over a century, he had merely substituted a different set of virtually independent lordlings, the Colonna conspicuous among them. For that reason his successor, Eugenius IV, a Venetian, had the whole task to do over again and by identical means. In both cases the enterprise meant wars involving most of Italy. By thus resorting to a policy of sheer opportunism so characteristic of fifteenth century Italian politics, these pontiffs set a precedent which would eventually transform the States of the Church into an Italian principate of first rank. The Renaissance popes would play their part upon the stage of European politics not as universal pontiffs but as Italian princes.

The pontificate of Pius II a decade later (1458-1464) illustrates a further step in this development. With the recovery of the Papal States now considerably advanced, Pius might have been expected to pursue his cherished aim of a Crusade against the Turks. None the less this project yielded place to more immediate concerns of the Italian political scene. Two contests occupied most of Pius' brief reign: on the one hand the long struggle with a recalcitrant papal vicar, Sigismondo Malatesta of Rimini, to recover lands wrested from the Church; on the other Pius' active participation in the wars fought over the Neapolitan succession. He has left us vivid accounts of both struggles in his own *Commentaries*. Sigismondo emerges as a monster of iniquity whose defiance of the Pope won for him the unique distinction of being canonized to hell! His defeat was accomplished only after a protracted and costly war.

The Neapolitan question illustrates the widening ramifications of papal territorial concerns. The Kingdom of Naples had since 1059 been a fief of the papacy, a relationship traditionally upheld by its French rulers and challenged by their Hohenstaufen — later Aragonese — rivals. As recently as 1443 Alfonso of Aragon, called "the Magnanimous," had overthrown the Angevin rule in Naples, thereby theoretically jeopardizing the papacy's age-long suzerainty over it. In actual fact, no complications ensued at the time: Alfonso sought and gained recognition by Pope Eugenius IV almost at once; the much harassed Eugenius, after initial resistance, was nothing loath to recognize as his vassal so able a ruler in the place of the faithless René of Anjou. His successor, Nicholas V, continued this precedent until his death in 1455.

By the time of Pius II's accession three years later, however, the serenity in Neapolitan relations had been rudely disturbed. Alfonso had revealed his designs upon Church lands which he hoped would find support by his erstwhile protégé, now Pope Calixtus III. Instead of support he met with furious opposition and threatened loss of his Kingdom. The crisis was averted by the death of both Alfonso and Calixtus in 1458. Thus when Pius II ascended the papal throne that year, the Neapolitan question in its old pattern had been revived. For Pius however the question was a practical one: would papal overlordship over Naples be best served by recognizing Alfonso's illegitimate son, Ferrante, the *de facto* ruler, incompetent and cruel tyrant though he was; or by supporting the one-time papal protégé, René of Anjou, in a losing cause? Pius chose the former course, exhibiting a sense of *Realpolitik* which his elaborate justification in the *Commentaries* fails to conceal.[1] His active participation in Ferrante's wars occupied most of his pontificate and involved much of Italy. The entry of Louis XI of France upon the scene in 1461 as protagonist of René's claims gave a European dimension to this Italian contest. As we shall see, Pius was able to make Naples a bargaining-point in return for Louis XI's revocation of the Pragmatic Sanction of Bourges, French symbol of the hated Conciliar principle. Thus not only have papal politics entered upon the wider European stage but are made to serve the goal of papal absolutism in the Church.

It was left for Sixtus IV who ascended the throne of St. Peter in 1471 to galvanize the haphazard achievements of his predecessors into a systematic program of consolidation. Sixtus had become convinced of the necessity of creating a militarily strong, centralized secular state on a level with the big

---

[1] E.g., his lengthy speech in Book V, (Smith College Studies in History, vol. XXX, p. 358 ff., trl. by F. A. Gragg, historical notes by L. C. Gabel, Northampton, Mass., 1947).

four in Italy if he was to command their respect or support. To that end he resorted to nepotism openly as an administrative policy, putting his numerous relatives in all strategic posts both in the Church and in the temporal government. The members of this obscure clan were of all sorts and kinds whose advancement lay in collaborating with the Pope rather than in independent ventures. The era of papal conquest and aggrandizement was thus launched by the Pope whose more famous nephew, Julius II, would carry it to its height.

Second only to the recovery of the States of the Church was the problem of the Council which hung over these fifteenth century popes like a sword of Damocles. The Councils had been called in response to a widespread demand for a healing of the Schism and reform of the Church. The Council of Constance, summoned in 1414 on the initiative of the Emperor Sigismund, had asserted the principle that a General Council of the Catholic Church received its authority directly from Christ and commanded the obedience of all men, including the Pope himself, in matters of faith and reform. The penalty of disobedience on the part of the Pope might, if necessary, be deposition. The decree *Frequens* provided for the calling of such Councils at regular intervals. A program of reform was of course the goal.

Reform, it should be noted, meant many things. It meant a reuniting of the Greek and other schismatic branches of the Christian Church with the Church of Rome. It meant the coming to grips with new heresy in Roman Catholic Christendom itself, notably the Hussite movement. It meant the reform of abuses in the Church which stemmed from a commercializing of its spiritual functions. Thus the very ambiguity of the term "reform" could be exploited for ulterior ends; and in a situation in which everybody needed to be reformed, it was much the easiest course to begin with someone or something else.

As viewed by the popes, the Conciliar doctrine was a proposition to be evaded, resisted, and at the first opportunity overthrown. It provoked a running battle between popes and councils until 1460 when Pius II annulled the hated decrees in his Bull *Execrabilis*. Of particular interest are the by-products of this Conciliar Theory. It not only stood in the way of papal absolutism within the Church as it was designed to do; but because it was linked with reform so urgently demanded throughout Europe, papal opposition to it was seen in many quarters as opposition to reform of the Church, as a betrayal of the office of Christ's Vicar on earth. From the Conciliar point of view, healing of the Schism, while indispensable to reform, was no guarantee of it, hence the desire to direct and control papal action. On the other hand, the Conciliar system was hardly a stimulus to papal initiative in matters of reform. Its effect was precisely the opposite. To the ambition of the popes to establish a strong Italian principate was added the determination to gain absolute authority within the Church. Inasmuch as the Conciliar Theory moreover proved a convenient form of blackmail in the hands of secular rulers bent on control over the Church in their realms, the political overtones of so-called reform could not be lost upon the papacy.   Ironically enough, councils and popes alike, in their conflict with each other, were but aggravating the religious crisis which would shortly bring an end to medieval religious unity.   In short, the popes of the fifteenth century in their efforts to recover lost power and prestige were swept along by deep and powerful currents ushering in a new era.   What appeared at first as the necessary prelude to the recovery of spiritual leadership would shortly become their accepted goal. Again, a closer glance at some specific examples will illustrate this facet of our subject.

Martin V's attitude to the hated Conciliar doctrine was one of studied neglect; when compelled to call a Council he lost no time in dissolving it on grounds of inefficiency.   Reform of the Church — especially of the papacy — was hardly a consuming passion of this Colonna pope.   He had plenty of spade-work to do more suited to his talents and tastes.

Yet his successor, Eugenius IV, a man of religious zeal and personal austerity long associated with monastic reform, proved even more recalcitrant. His stormy pontificate was one long battle with the Council of Basel in the course of which both parties went to extremes, even to the extent of a new schism.   At the point of extreme tension Eugenius resorted to the strategy of transferring the Council to Ferrara[2] where the union of the Greek and Roman Churches would come first on the agenda of reform.   By this act Eugenius scored a double victory: he precipitated the showdown with Basel which was already imminent, thus enabling him to declare its existence at an end; he won for the papacy the credit for bringing about the union of the Churches — a project dear to the hearts of the Fathers at Basel.   Actually it turned out to be a hollow victory: the Conciliar Theory remained intact, the union of the Churches proved ephemeral; nor did the "rump" still in session at Basel obediently give up the ghost.

Certain parallels suggest themselves between this earnest Venetian pope and his twentieth-century fellow Venetian, the late Pope John XXIII.   Both pontiffs called Councils to heal schism in Christendom, to take steps to restore unity to the Church by re-examining the differences that separated the churches.   But on closer inspection the resemblance fades.   The real initiative in the fifteenth century had come from the Eastern Emperor and the Greek Church in a desperate move to win the aid of the West against the Turks.   It comes as no surprise, therefore, that the union achieved at Ferrara-Florence hardly outlived the return journey of the Greek delegates.   And so, reformer

---

[2] Transferred shortly from Ferrara to Florence because of an outbreak of plague. Since Eugenius had assumed the full expenses of the Greek delegation, the selection of Florence was no doubt influenced by Cosimo'de'Medici's offer of assistance to the financially embarrassed Pope.   The move, of course, was profitable to Florence as well.

though he was, Eugenius had done little more to advance the cause of reform than had Martin V.

The use of the Conciliar Theory for purposes of political blackmail is best illustrated from the history of the so-called Pragmatic Sanction of Bourges. This was a royal proclamation of Charles VII of France in 1438 which greatly restricted the right of the papacy to collect revenues in France and to appoint to French benefices. In order to put teeth into these limitations on papal prerogatives in France, the Conciliar doctrine was incorporated in the Pragmatic Sanction where it enjoyed a healthy existence for many years. A situation tailored to bring this instrument into full play came about in the pontificate of Pius II some twenty years later. Thinking the moment had come to annul the objectionable conciliar decrees, Pius did so in no uncertain terms in the Bull *Execrabilis* of the year 1460. Henceforth it would constitute heresy and treason to appeal to a Council over the head of a pope. In conformity with this papal decree it now fell to the King of France to revoke the Pragmatic Sanction of Bourges.

From the ailing King Charles VII nothing was to be hoped; but the new monarch, Louis XI, who came to the throne the next year saw here a chance to drive a shrewd bargain. Louis on his part desired the Pope's recognition of the French claim to the Kingdom of Naples, a papal fief then held, as we have seen, by the Aragonese King Ferrante. To gain this Louis XI felt he had a perfect *quid pro quo* in the desired revocation of the Pragmatic Sanction. But Louis had met his match. The diplomatic jockeying between King and Pope makes enthralling reading as Pius tells the tale in his *Commentaries*. Having been encouraged in his expectations regarding Naples, Louis XI immediately revoked the Pragmatic Sanction of Bourges, only to find that Pius was not yet prepared to abandon Ferrante. It was necessary, so Pius contended, to continue to recognize Ferrante as *de facto* ruler until such time as the restoration of peace would permit an examination of the claims of both parties. Meanwhile the Pope continued actively to support Ferrante in his wars. Louis XI's reflections may easily be conjectured. At all events the obnoxious Conciliar doctrine was now officially dead even though burial was not to take place until 1516 in the Concordat of Bologna.

In sum, the papacy has entered the game of international politics, not as a universal authority but as one political power against or among others. The pope no longer even pretends to exercise temporal power outside his own domains which by Sixtus IV's pontificate have been welded into a strong secular state. To gain their ends, whether political or ecclesiastical, the popes will resort to Machiavellian strategy in separate deals with individual monarchs. This is modern statecraft.

Mending political fences was inseparable from repairing the papal treasury. This involved setting in motion the machinery of a highly organized tax system which was a legacy from the Avignonese popes — a machinery creaking under the weight of a mushrooming officialdom and thrown out of gear by the disorders of the schism. These activities form a chapter in the history of the Reformation which brought medieval religious unity to an end. We are concerned primarily with one facet of this Avignonese legacy which came down to the fifteenth century popes unimpaired, the close link between the fiscal system of the Church and the new capitalism. This connection was one which profoundly changed the character of the medieval papacy in any event, and in the context of fifteenth century developments took on new dimensions.

It will be recalled that the popes at Avignon had found the far-flung banking facilities of Italian merchants a convenient instrument for the transmitting of taxes collected in distant parts as well as in the traffic in ecclesiastical benefices. Neither the economic disasters of the fourteenth century nor the Schism at its close affected this relationship. The Medici bank, founded by Giovanni di Bicci de' Medici and famous in Florentine history, began in the late fourteenth century as a Rome bank to handle funds for the papal treasury, following the Curia in its rounds. Even after the transfer of its seat to Florence in 1397 the records show the Rome branch to continue as the chief source of profits. In his recent study of the Medici bank Professor de Roover[3] points out that from 1422 on the papal court "was seeking to invest rather than to borrow"[4] and surmises that the move of banking headquarters to Florence may have been influenced by the desire to invest surplus funds from the Rome branch.[5] Only five years later the first of a succession of Medici partnerships for the production of woolen cloth was set up. In 1427 Pope Martin V is listed as a depositor *a discrezione,* i.e., one whose deposits were available for investment, which is to say, to earn interest. The Church teachings regarding usury belonged in practice to an era that was past.

Succeeding pontificates show an increasingly important rôle of business in papal politics. Pope Eugenius IV, as we have seen, was undoubtedly influenced by considerations of financial aid from Cosimo de' Medici in transferring the Council of Ferrara to Florence in 1439. The discovery in 1460 of alum mines at Tolfa in the States of the Church provided occasion for the direct participation of the papacy in a cartel for the mining and marketing of this highly important commodity. Nothing less than a monopoly would suffice; ecclesiastical censures were brought to bear upon purchasers of Turkish alum while competition from Christian rivals was dealt with by cartel agreements with them. Here again the Medici Bank with its extensive commercial network soon played a leading rôle. The ramifications of the alum

[3] R. de Roover, *The Rise and Fall of the Medici Bank,* Cambridge, Mass., 1962. I am indebted to this work for the details which follow.
[4] *Ibid.,* p. 38.
[5] *Ibid.,* p. 99.

monopoly — both diplomatic and financial — were European-wide and lasted on down through the century. It was to figure in the circumstances leading to the famous Pazzi Conspiracy in 1478 when Sixtus IV transferred the alum contract to the Pazzi; this rival of the Medici had but recently supplanted them as bankers to the Curia. The outcome of these strained relations between the Pope and the Medici, as is well known, did not stop short of assassination and war between the papacy and Florence.

From these scattered instances it is readily apparent that business and politics went hand in hand for these fifteenth century popes no less than for their secular counterparts. The attempt of Pius II and Paul II to justify the alum monopoly as a means of raising revenue for a Crusade fails to conceal the true nature of what was taking place; before the century closes the need to justify such procedures will have ceased to be felt.

So far I have tried to show that the recovery of Rome and the Papal States led in the end to the creation of a frankly secular Italian state bent on aggrandizement. And that the threat offered to papal authority by the General Councils drew the ecclesiastical policy of the popes away from any interest they may have had in reform and hence from their traditional rôle as spiritual head of Christendom. There remains to be considered a new kind of bid by the popes for world prestige through the patronage of arts and letters — the acknowledged goal of making Rome the *cultural* capital of Christendom.

This goal too was the product of new circumstances. Neither Martin V nor Eugenius IV, unlike as they were, had time or taste for the cultural developments of their day. Yet Martin liked pomp and elegance; he liked the special skills offered by the humanists as secretaries, as orators for special occasions. Moreover he was trying to make Rome habitable. One cannot dig in Rome without coming upon the traces of ancient as well as of early Christian Rome. Little wonder then that a humanist like Poggio Bracciolini, irreverent author of bawdy tales and enthusiast for classical antiquity, a papal secretary under Martin V, hailed that pontificate as a Golden Age for men of letters. Or that Martin's activities in restoring Rome took place to the accompaniment of intense archaeological interest in ancient monuments.

Eugenius too had other things than the classics to worry about but he had even greater need of humanists who knew Greek to serve him as interpreters in his Council to unite the Greek and Latin churches. Driven from Ferrara by an outbreak of the plague, this Council found hospitality in Cosimo de' Medici's Florence, the intellectual and artistic nerve-center of Renaissance Italy. Although the union of the Churches achieved there was short-lived as we have seen, this gathering of Greek and Latin scholars in the intellectual atmosphere of Florence gave a tremendous impetus to the study of Greek classics, in particular to the study of Plato. It was through the enthusiastic Greek Platonist, George Gemisthos Plethon, prominent at the Council, that Cosimo himself was inspired to found a Platonic academy in his own city, sponsoring the education of his physician's promising son, Marsiglio Ficino, in Greek studies to lead in the enterprise. Pope Eugenius had all unwittingly furthered an interest which was to have a profound influence on the intellectual history of Europe.

One can sense the atmosphere of the papal court at this time from a treatise by a young humanist in the service of Pope Eugenius at the Council of Ferrara-Florence. From the pen of Lapo da Castiglionchio[6] we have a *Dialogue* setting forth the reasons why the papal court was of all places the most ideal for a man of letters. The dialogue takes place between a bishop of more conservative views and Lapo himself, a humanist. We learn from Lapo that the papal court offers advantages no other court can give. To the scholar it offers unique opportunities for study, for meeting learned men from all parts of the world in every field of knowledge. No, he is not referring to canonists or theologians, or mathematicians and others who may lend it dignity perhaps but whose subjects are neither of benefit nor of interest nowadays. Rather has he in mind the Greek and Italian humanists — Leon Battista Alberti towering above them all. For a writer, Lapo goes on to say, the papal court is a sure road to fame, commanding as it does a world audience. There is always an abundance of good company, witty conversation, complete freedom — no topic forbidden. And such food! And what sights! At present when East and West are met for the union of the Churches, one can see long beards, short beards, painted eyebrows, skull-caps, turbans and bejewelled mitres — melancholy itself must give way to laughter before sights so ridiculous. And where else is the service of religion performed with such pomp, such magnificence of color and sound?

When the Bishop in turn ventures to remark that Christ and His disciples were poor and enjoined a life of humility and self-denial, Lapo confidently asserts that no age can live by the standards of the past. What was appropriate for Christ and the disciples would be entirely out of place today. If the pope went about barefoot or riding on an ass, he would be the laughingstock of the world! What our times demand is not less wealth for the Church but *more;* to the service of religion should be brought all that numbers, pomp and splendour can give.

I have drawn upon Lapo at some length not only because he reveals the attitudes and criteria of the younger set at Eugenius' court, but because these are prophetic of what was to come.

We have only to wait for Eugenius' successor, Nicholas V, for the beginning of what the Catholic historian, Pastor, called "the golden age of humanists". Nicholas V, the gentle pope, frail of body but keen of mind

<hr/>

[6] Nephew of the more famous Lapo da Castiglionchio, friend of Petrarch. The text of the *Dialogus super excellencia et dignitate curie Romane* etc. was published under the title of *Eine Humanistische Schilderung der Kurie aus dem Jahre 1438* by Richard Scholz, Rome, 1913.

and generous of heart, was himself an avid lover of books. He once said, while still a tutor earning his way, if he ever were rich, he would spend his wealth on two things: buildings and books. And so it was. A new St. Peter's, a new Vatican, a new Vatican Library were among his hopes, only the last actually realized in his pontificate. It seemed to be Nicholas' aim, like that of the twentieth century Pope John XXIII, to open the windows of the Church to let in fresh air. For Nicholas it meant calling to his court the ablest humanists of his day not merely to serve as secretaries but to produce works of scholarship, to translate Greek classics. He could even read the obscenities of a Filelfo and applaud the man's genius. Place was found in his service for a Lorenzo Valla who had levelled a devastating criticism at papal temporal power and whose speculations skirted the edge of heresy. Architects and painters were summoned to build and to adorn. Nicholas V's own words on his death-bed are eloquent:[8]

> I have so reformed and so confirmed the Holy Roman Church which I found devastated by war and oppressed by debts, that I have eradicated schism and won back her cities and castles. I have not only freed her from her debts but erected magnificent fortresses for her defense: . . . I have adorned her with glorious buildings and decked her with pearls and precious stones. I have provided her with costly books and tapestry, with gold and silver vessels and splendid vestments. And I did not collect all these treasures by grasping avarice and simony. In all things I was liberal, in building, in the purchase of books, in the constant transcription of Greek and Latin MSS and in the remuneration of learned men. All this has been bestowed upon me by the Divine Grace, owing to the continued peace of the Church during my pontificate.

To restore Rome to her ancient place as the center of culture — this was his acknowledged goal; a goal in which a *new* Rome and the revival of ancient Rome were but two sides of a single coin. This is a new bid for world prestige.

What becomes evident is that Italian humanism was not just a literary cult ablaze with enthusiasm for classical authors and elegant Latinity. Out of its renewed contact with antiquity grew a consuming interest in all that the classical past had stood for. In a young humanist like Lapo we see a conscious rejection of old-fashioned standards, a concern for fame, a secular turn of mind. At the Florentine Academy founded by Cosimo de' Medici, philosophers no longer tried to reconcile Plato with Christianity but Christianity with Plato; at Padua a new look at Aristotle would pretty well put the burden of proof on Christian doctrine. A new image of man emerges — one which would have raised even classical eyebrows. Rational man was seen as the miniature of God in his creative potential; sin was but a misguided

---

[7] *History of the Popes,* vol. II, p. 194, ed. F. I. Antrobus, London, 1923.
[8] *Ibid.,* p. 312.

approach to God. It was a *Weltanschauung* almost fit for a space-age! Certainly it suited the character of the Renaissance popes who were both its patrons and its representatives.

Succeeding popes implemented Nicholas V's dreams for Rome according to their individual interests. In the person of Pius II a humanist ascended the throne of St. Peter. Here is the egoistic but genial self-made man of letters, traveller, orator, lover of people and of the out-of-doors; urbane, critical, astute. For him the interest in classical antiquity amounted to a passion. His voluminous writings already covered a wide range of subjects, including one or two racy best-sellers which caused him no small embarrassment as Pope. Pius was not so much the patron of Renaissance humanism as its personification. *He* was the papacy; the papal court was where *he* was. And for this inveterate traveller that meant almost anywhere in Italy except Rome itself. When the heat of summer made Rome intolerable, Pius and his court took to the hills where Signatura might be ". . . held in the woods under one tree or another by the sweet murmur of the stream . . ." and Consistory with the Cardinals "under the chestnuts," while embassies might be heard in the meadow.[9]

A good clue to his complex personality and to the spirit of his times is provided in the Preface Pius wrote to his *Commentaries*:

> . . .pleasure in the glory of the present sustains the most brilliant minds and cheers and refreshes the heart of man even more than the hope of celestial life. This is especially true of the Pope of Rome. After his death, Envy will be still and true report will rise again to number Pius among the illustrious popes.[10]

Here in every sense of the term was a humanist. The religious impulse which dominated the last year of his life came too late to leave its impress upon his pontificate.

Turning once more — and finally — to Sixtus IV, this pope of humble origin, we find that the creation of a brilliant Renaissance court is as methodically pursued as the creation of a powerful military state; one is as indispensable as the other. In the patronage of art Rome owed more to Sixtus and his relatives than to any other. Indeed his greatest contribution on both counts lay in elevating to the cardinalate one of those many relatives — his nephew Giuliano delle Rovere, the future Pope Julius II — and putting him in charge of the artistic projects of his pontificate; Julius II in whom the High Renaissance would see the fulfillment of Sixtus' bold aspirations: Julius the *warrior* pope who was to make the papal state the most powerful state in Italy, a state to be reckoned with in the arena of European politics; Julius the

---

[9] *Commentaries of Pius II*, Bk. IX, Smith College Studies in History vol. XXXV, p. 571.   V
[10] *Ibid.*, vol. XXII.

builder under whom the new Rome would be the envy and pride of Western Christendom.

In sum, the revival of Rome as the seat of a reunited Church in the fifteenth century took place in circumstances that were new, in an intellectual climate that was new. Behind it lay a century of exile and schism, visible manifestations of the dissolution of the medieval scheme of things then in process; in the making was the papacy of the High Renaissance — builders of a new Rome, architects of a powerul Italian state, presiding over Italy's cultural zenith as she hastened to her political doom. This is no longer the medieval papacy; nor yet the papacy in the divided Christendom of modern times; it is the papacy of the Renaissance.

THE CONTRIBUTION OF MARTIN V TO THE
REBUILDING OF ROME, 1420 - 1431

Ruth W. Kennedy

Professor Emeritus of Art,

Smith College

It is gratifying to me to be collaborating once again with Miss Gabel and to be finding with her ways in which history can shed light on artistic problems and ways in which art can illumine history.

We have agreed in this symposium to "reconsider the Renaissance." For an art historian, the most obvious thing to do in dealing with the fifteenth century re-building of Rome would be to concentrate on the papacies of Nicholas V and Sixtus IV, because these two were responsible for more buildings, more paintings and more illuminated manuscripts than any other popes of the century. But it seems worthwhile to reconsider the rôle of Martin V who re-established the papal residence in Rome in the fall of 1419 and died there in the winter of 1431.[1] We shall find him the initiator of many policies which were developed more fully by his successors.

Martin was born a Roman noble. Modern research has discredited the cherished belief of the Colonna family that their ancestors were patricians of the Roman Empire and has failed to trace their presence in Rome before the ninth century, but, nonetheless, when Martin was elected at Constance in 1417, the Colonnas had a long family tradition as Romans. They probably owned more land inside and outside Rome than any other noble family, and it was usually true that some imposing ruins still stood on their various properties. For instance, on the Quirinal above their principal town house, one could still see in Martin's time the massive remains of Aurelian's temple of the Sun.[2] Images of notable earlier Colonnas were still numerous on mediaeval buildings. For instance, the Senator Giovanni Colonna is shown adoring the Virgin in a mosaic which is still in the church of the Araceli on the Capitoline hill. In 1420 the façade of S. Maria Maggiore still bore the now lost images of the Cardinals Giacomo and Pietro Colonna who were represented as donors of the mosaic which tells the mediaeval legend of the miraculous fall of summer snow which outlined for Pope Liberius the Virgin's plan for her greatest church. Turriti's mosaic of the *Coronation of the Virgin* on the chancel arch still shows us at the lower left how Cardinal

---

[1] M. Creighton, *A History of the Papacy from the Great Schism to the Sack of Rome,* New York, 1905, II, pp. 131 ff. gives an account of Martin's papacy.

[2] For the location of the Colonna properties near SS. Apostoli cf. the map of Rome published by Bufalini May 26, 1551 and reproduced in F. Ehrle, *Piante e vedute di Roma,* etc., Città del Vaticano, 1956; also figure 10.

[27]

Giacomo looked in 1295 when he paid for the decoration of this famous early Christian basilica.[3]   It was a Colonna who was Petrarch's favorite companion in his rambles about Rome which culminated at sunset on top of the Baths of Diocletian.   There the two friends talked together of the great past of the city spread out before their eyes and spoke of their dreams that the Romans of their own time might be inspired to begin a new age of greatness.[4]   Petrarch's concept of the instructive value of the spectacle of Rome is often thereafter repeated in the phrase "How great Rome was these ruins teach."   For example, it appears above the two ruined arches in the frontispiece of Serlio's *Third Book on Architecture* as if it were a genuine inscription.[5]

Thus the new pope would have in his blood Petrarch's belief in Rome as the *caput mundi,* and he would be equally aware that the Church must return to the tomb of its founder, St. Peter, from whom its authority was derived.[6]

How significant a figure St. Peter seemed at this time we may deduce from the powerful images of the Apostle created by Masaccio on the walls of the Brancacci Chapel in S. Maria del Carmine in Florence, and, we may remind ourselves, the dedication of his family's chapel to the founder of the Church coincides with the diplomatic mission to Florence in 1425 of one of Martin's most able adjutants, the Cardinal Brancacci.[7]   Further confirmation of Peter's importance comes from Donatello's relief, now in the Victoria and Albert Museum in London, which has been plausibly identified as a part of the original marble altar of the Brancacci Chapel.[8]   (figure 1)   In this relief Peter's spiritual authority is being conferred upon him directly by Christ in the moment of His ascension into Heaven, an episode which, while not literally taken from the closing linens of the Gospel of St. John, is exactly in accord with its implications.   This is clear from the tapestry which a sixteenth century successor of Martin's, Leo X, asked Raphael to design for the central chapel of the Vatican Palace, the Sistina, where the Risen Christ's charge to Peter, "Feed my sheep," as quoted by St. John, shows the Apostle with the keys of authority already in his hand.   Still another proof comes from Masaccio's predella for his Pisan altarpiece of 1426.[9]   (figure 2)   We

---

[3] A. Muñoz, *Roma di Dante,* Rome, 1921, pp. 201-208; M. Armellini, *Le Chiese di Roma,* etc., Rome, 1942, I, pp. 281 ff.

[4] P. de Nolhac, *Petrarch and the Ancient World,* Boston, 1907, pp. 20-22.

[5] Published in Venice 1540. This phrase had often been used before this time, and probably even antedates Petrarch.

[6] *Memoirs of a Renaissance Pope,* trans. F. A. Gragg, ed. L. C. Gabel, New York, 1959, pp. 83-84 for the arguments of Cardinal Branda Castiglione about the necessity of establishing the papacy in Rome.

[7] Cf. U. Procacci, "Sulla cronologia delle opere di Masaccio e di Masolino tra il 1425 e il 1428," *Rivista d'arte,* 1953, pp. 3-55 for full information on the chronology of the chapel.

[8] J. Pope-Hennessy, *Donatello's Relief of the Ascension,* London, 1949; H. W. Janson, *The Sculpture of Donatello,* Princeton, 1957, I, pp. 93-94.

[9] M. Salmi, *Masaccio,* Rome, n.d., p. 90.

see St. Peter crucified in the fashion which Flavio Biondo says was common in his day — "between the two *metas*."[10] One *meta* from the Circus of Nero was still in existence at this time, long since denuded of the gilded bronze covering given it by Caligula. During these very years in which we are interested, antiquarians began wrangling among themselves as to whether the phrase "between the two *metas*" applied to the platform in Nero's circus with its central obelisk and two terminal *metas*, or whether the phrase should really be interpreted as referring to a spot half-way between the solitary remaining *meta* of the circus and the other *meta*, the so-called "sudans," near the Arch of Constantine half the city of Rome away. The continuous belief in the Neronian obelisk as the true site of the saint's martyrdom can be deduced from the intention of both Nicholas V and Paul II to move the great monolith from its position at the side of the basilica of St. Peter's to the piazza in front of the church. Neither pope fulfilled his dream; it was left to Sixtus V to accomplish the task in 1586.[11] However, the dissident view was still strong enough in 1503 to induce Ferdinand and Isabella of Spain to hire Bramante to build his beautiful *tempietto* on the alleged half-way spot. It was reckoned as being exactly in the middle of the courtyard of a church on the Janiculum which had received the advocation of S. Pietro in Montorio some time before.[12]

We can only say that it took a high resolve to set about rebuilding Rome in 1420. All the contemporary writers agree that the city presented a sorry spectacle. Without the papacy, its very reason for existence was fast disappearing, and what we read of its delapidation makes us feel that, had the popes remained in Avignon, Rome would be as lost to us today as Nineveh and Tyre. Drawings which were made by a pupil of Ghirlandaio's half a century later, for instance, show enough desolation and acumulated rubbish to indicate to us how tremendous the task of rebuilding proved to be.[13]

Martin appears to have set about this task in a thoroughly reasonable way. While he was still in Florence, he arranged with the Medici bank for credit to pay for the rehabilitation of the Vatican palace which had often sheltered his predecessors.[14] Pope Martin did not remain in the Vatican palace for long, but soon moved to one of the Colonna houses in the Piazza

---

[10] *Roma Ristaurata . . di Biondo da Forli*, trans. L. Fauno, Venice, 1558, p. 11. Biondo's original Latin text was composed in Rome in 1444-46 and dedicated to Eugenius IV. Note a contemporary representation of St. Peter's crucifixion "between the two *metas*" in a manuscript in the Biblioteca Laurenziana, Ms. Conv. Soppr. 457, f. 361v., no. 350, p. 228, M. Salmi, *Mostra storica nazionale della miniatura*, Florence, 1953.

[11] B. Dibner, *Moving the Obelisks*, Norwalk, Conn., 1952. Cf. also C. Huelsen, "Il circo di Nerone al Vaticano," *Miscellanea Ariani, Milan*, 1910 and E. Nash, "Circus und Obelisk," *Römische Mitteilungen*, 1957.

[12] M. Armellini, *op. cit.*, II, pp. 809-11.

[13] H. Egger, *Codex Escurialensis*, Vienna, 1906.

[14] E. Müntz, "Les arts à la cour des papes," *Bibliothèque des écoles françaises d'Athènes et de Rome*, 1878, I, p. 6. This same volume also provides complete documentary information on the patronage of the arts by Martin's successors.

SS. Apostoli.   His fifteenth century successors, however, recognized the symbolic value of this venerable residence, called since the fifth century the *Domus Aguliae,* or Palace of the Obelisk,[15] and they not only restored it as their official dwelling, but they added to it Fra Angelico's Cappella Niccolina, the "Stanze" frescoed by Castagno and Piero della Francesca, the library with its frescoes by Ghirlandaio and Melozzo da Forli, and, most impressive of all, the Sistine Chapel decorated for Sixtus IV by the most eminent painters of the later Quattrocento under the direction of Botticelli.

Again, even before Martin reached Rome, he began preparing suitable liturgical vessels and vestments, as the nature of his office required him to do.   The eminent Florentine sculptor and goldsmith, Lorenzo Ghiberti, was asked to make a mitre with six golden figures and a jewelled button for Martin's ceremonial cope. His successor, Eugenius IV, was to call on Ghiberti for an even more sumptuous tiara.[16]   Ghiberti's fame was not sufficient to preserve these treasures from the pawnshop and the crucible, but we can, perhaps, see again one of Martin's splendid copes in the garment worn by his patron saint in Masolino's panel from the altarpiece which this pope gave to S. Maria Maggiore sometime between 1424 and 1428.[17]   (figure 3) The golden Ms of more or less Gothic form would refer equally well to the saint and to the picture's donor.   The archives of the Vatican abound in references to sumptuous liturgical vestments ordered by all the popes who followed Martin.   It was probably one of the jewelled tiaras and brocaded copes in the wardrobe of Nicholas V which Fra Angelico gave to Pope Sixtus II in his fresco of *St. Lawrence receiving the Treasures of the Church,* since we know that the features of Nicholas were bestowed on the unrecorded visage of the third century protagonist.[18]   The recent restoration of the Cappella Niccolina has revealed a dado of simulated brocade, not unlike that frescoed by Botticelli on the lower walls of the Sistine Chapel, and we know from the expenses of the Camera, that Nicholas and most of his immediate successors gave pretty continuous employment to German embroiderers and Flemish tapestry weavers.   Almost nothing remains, but an altar frontal still in the Treasury of S. Francesco at Assisi, which shows Sixtus kneeling in adoration before the founder of the order to which he had belonged at the beginning of his ecclesiastical career, looks as if it had been designed by Antonio Pollaiolo and executed by the German embroiderers who had worked

[15] C. Cecchelli, *Il Vaticano,* Rome, 1927, pp. 68-69.
[16] E. Müntz, *loc. cit.;* R. Krautheimer and T. Krautheimer-Hess, *Lorenzo Ghiberti,* Princeton, 1956, pp. 5, 13, 67.
[17] K. Clark, "An Early Quattrocento Triptych from S. Maria Maggiore," *Burlington Magazine,* vol. 98, 1951, pp. 272-280; M. Salmi, "Gli scomparti della pala di Santa Maria Maggiore," *Commentari,* 1952, pp. 14-21; H. Marceau, *John G. Johnson Collection,* Philadelphia, 1953, p. 23; cf. pp. 51 ff. in the article by U. Procacci cited in n. 7 for suggestions as to the dating of the altarpiece.
[18] R. Langton Douglas, *Fra Angelico,* London, 1902, p. 128.

with the Florentine artist before he went to Rome to make the tomb of Sixtus IV about 1484.[19]

Naturally, there was nothing new in ordering jewels and copes from the most famous of craftsmen. The breathtaking assemblage of vestments made for Boniface VIII and now in the Caetani palace at Anagni, Nicholas IV's famous cope in *opus anglicanum* at Ascoli Piceno and many other ecclesiastical treasures are sufficient evidence that the popes of the Middle Ages were well aware of the value and propriety of beautiful ceremonial garments. Martin was, therefore, only following a hallowed tradition.

Much the same can be said of Martin's activity as a builder. He began with the obvious essentials. In 1425 he revived the office of supervisor of the streets of Rome. He was primarily interested in getting them cleaned so that traffic could proceed with greater ease especially in that Holy Year. Records also exist of his subsequent repairs to two bridges over the Tiber, Constantine's Ponte Molle and the Ponte S. Maria — which since the late sixteenth century we have been obliged to call the Ponte Rotto. Although these decisions show Martin's practical wisdom in dealing with an administrative problem and were by no means original ideas, they were to have far-reaching consequences. The excellence and durability of Roman roads very much impressed the men of the fifteenth century accustomed as they were to much more casual thoroughfares. A well-paved street which excited considerable admiration was found several feet below the ground when the foundations of the Palazzo Venezia were dug in 1455, and Leon Battista Alberti, in devoting two chapters to city planning in his *Treatise on Architecture* which was dedicated to Nicholas V in 1452, mentions with special approval the still visible highway from Rome to Ostia.[20]

Martin's successors followed his example almost without exception, repairing bridges, clearing streets and creating piazzas. Eugenius, in demolishing the "dirty taverns" which huddled around the Pantheon, came across two granite lions from the nearby Temple of Isis which were presently set up in the open space in front of the church on either side of a huge porphyry sarcophagus. (figure 4) Visitors to Rome were evidently much taken with these relics, for we find Giovanni Rucellai, who saw the lions in the piazza during the Holy Year of 1450, ordering Alberti to copy them for the portico of his parish church of S. Pancrazio in Florence.[21] Prince James of Portugal, who was the titular cardinal of St. Eustace just around the corner from the Pantheon, was buried in a marble replica of the porphyry sarcophagus in the tomb which Bernardo and Antonio Rosellino executed for him in S. Mini-

[19] E. Müntz, *op. cit.*, p. 16 ff.; A. Sabatini, *Antonio e Piero del Pollaiolo*, Florence, 1944, pp. 14 ff. and Pl. XXIIb.
[20] Bk. IV, Chaps. V and VI.
[21] M. Armellini, *op. cit.*, I, pp. 589 ff.; H. Egger, *op. cit.*, I, p. 116.

ato al Monte in the 1460's.[22]   Other piazzas were similarly adorned. Cardinal Pietro Barbo, who was to become Pope Paul II, brought to the open space before S. Marco, a porphyry sarcophagus from S. Costanza and a large marble fragment, affectionately called by the Romans "Madama Lucrezia."[23] These were small beginnings, but they constitute the nucleus of modern ideas on city planning which was already being advocated by such fifteenth century architects as Alberti, Filarete and Francesco di Giorgio.   And these incipient ideas led eventually to the complete alteration of the topography of Rome in the late sixteenth century.

We are told that Martin was very effective in restoring order in Rome and in discouraging invasiaon from without.   We might, therefore, expect to find him strengthening the walls, gates and towers of the city. The records seem to indicate that this was the work of his successors, particularly of Eugenius and Nicholas.[24] Perhaps the best idea we can form of the protective crenellated walls which Nicholas rebuilt around the city can be found in the fresco of the *Stoning of St. Stephen* which the pope's old Florentine friend Fra Angelico painted for his private chapel.

Of course, it was equally important for Martin to keep in mind the function of Rome as the capital of Christendom where religious services must constantly be performed at the tombs of its martyrs.   During the millenium since the first Christian churches were built, it had often been necessary to repair them.   Since Martin saw so many Roman churches in an almost hopeless state of collapse, he chose for repair those with the greatest historical and spiritual significance, that is, the great pilgrim basilicas, St. Peter's, the cathedral of the Lateran and S. Maria Maggiore.   This policy was invariably followed by Martin's successors, Eugenius ordering from Filarete the bronze doors for St. Peter's, undertaking the restoration of the basilicas of S. Paolo fuori le Mura and of S. Maria in Trastevere, while Nicholas was to concentrate on the renewal of the Vatican complex and the Borgo Leonina which had been originally developed by the Carolingian pope, Leo III. It, therefore, seems appropriate, since Nicholas evidently wished Angelico's frescoes in his private chapel to refer discreetly to his own activities, that St. Peter should be shown there as administering the sacrament to St. Stephen in a building which is obviously an Early Christian basilica and from an altar housed in a tabernacle of an Early Christian type.

Today, we call the only great building which has survived all but intact from Roman Imperial times, the Pantheon, but its proper designation since the eighth century has been S. Maria ad Martyres.   It is, therefore, symbolic

[22] F. Hartt, G. Corti and C. Kennedy, *The Chapel of the Cardinal of Portugal,* University of Pennsylvania Press, Philadelphia, Pa. (in press).
[23] R. Weiss, *Un umanista veneziano: Papa Paolo II,* Civiltà Veneziana, Saggi 4, Venice, 1958, p. 24.
[24] E. Müntz, *op. cit.,* pp. 68 ff. using Gianozzo Manetti's contemporary biography of Nicholas V.

of the triumph of Christianity over paganism and, as such, deserved the attention which Martin gave it.   He had time only to begin the restitution of its
lead roof tiles.   His successor, Eugenius, carried the work much farther as
we have already seen.   In roofing over S. Stefano Rotondo in the 1450's,
Nicholas V was pursuing the same policy — choosing for repair an ancient
building which had been converted to Christian use.

Let us look more attentively at Martin's three major restorations.   At
St. Peter's his work seems to have been confined to propping up the tottering
portico of the venerable Contantinian basilica and to tidying up its mediaeval
mosaics.   His problem at the Lateran was much more difficult.   The basilica
had twice been seriously damaged by fire during the Avignonese exile.
Martin's biographers credit him with erecting certain antique columns and
with laying down the present marble pavement.[25] (figure 5)   Eventually his
own tomb was set up in the portico of the Lateran in the company of those
of many earlier bishops of Rome.   It was too much to hope that the Lateran
could be completely renovated during a single papacy, and later on, we find
Pius II going to inspect the repairs he was having made to the roof.[26]

With all his solicitude for his titular church, one regrets having to admit
that Martin specifically told his agents to use marbles from abandoned
churches for the Lateran's new pavement.[27] Alas, this policy was also followed
by his successors.   The humanist Nicholas permitted the spoliation of the
Colisseum of travertine blocks for the new apse of St. Peter's and we could
cite many more such melancholy examples.

More than structural repairs seemed to Martin to be needed at the Lateran.
The walls between and above the windows needed ornamentation with appropriate images if he was to follow traditional practise   There was no one
in Rome whom the pope could call on for the purpose.   Over a century
before, Giotto's master, the Roman Cavallini had been an excellent local
painter and mosaicist, but throughout the whole fifteenth century there simply
was no Roman-born painter above the level of the anemic Antoniazzo, whose
Annunciation was set up in S. Maria sopra Minerva in the time of Sixtus, nor
was there any sculptor more gifted than the mediocre Paolo Romano, whose
statues of the two Princes of the Church were placed by Pius at the foot of
the new marble stairway to St. Peter's which replaced the old worn steps.[28]
Martin was therefore forced to look outside of Rome for his painter.   He
gave the Lateran commission to Gentile da Fabriano, then famous enough to
deserve the tears of the Muses at his death, if we may believe the inscription
on his tomb.[29] Pope and painter had apparently met at Brescia as long before

[25] E. Müntz, *op. cit.*, pp. 14 ff. following Platina's biography of Martin of 1474.
[26] *Memoirs of a Renaissance Pope*, ed. cit., p. 323.
[27] E. Müntz, *op. cit.*, p. 5.
[28] *Memoirs of a Renaissance Pope, ed. cit.*, p. 254.
[29] For the Lateran frescoes see E. Müntz, *op. cit.*, pp. 39 ff. and B. Degenhart,
Pisanello, Chiantore, n. d.; for the original appearance of the nave see L. von Pastor.
Die Stadt Rom zu Ende der Renaissance, Freiburg, 1925, p. 124.

as 1418, but it was then too soon to make ambitious plans. Gentile actually
began the decoration of the Lateran only in 1427. He represented several
prophets and certain scenes from the Life of St. John which were left unfinished at his death a year later. Unhappily, these frescoes are gone, scraped
away in the Baroque restoration of the church. We regret them all the more
since we know that Michelangelo said of the painter's Roman work, "Gentle
in hand as well as name" — and in those days the adjective "gentle" was
really the equivalent of "noble."[30] The Quaratesi altarpiece, done in Florence
just before Gentile's departure for Rome, probably gives us the best idea of
what we have lost — splendid figures in the final Gothic style. (figure 6).
When Eugenius followed Martin, he called Gentile's pupil Pisanello from
Verona to finish the master's work. These frescoes too have gone, but we
still possess Pisanello's portrait of the Emperor Sigismond, painted when he
came to Rome to be crowned by Eugenius in 1432.[31]

Martin advised his cardinals to follow his example in repairing their
titular churches and their adjacent palaces. Cardinal Branda da Castiglione
accordingly summoned Masolino and Masaccio, who had been working together in Florence for the Cardinal Brancacci's family and gave them the task
of adorning a chapel on the upper level of his Early Christian church of S.
Clemente. Cardinal Branda had already shown himself energetic in the cause
of restoration, for even before he began the work at S. Clemente about 1427
or 1428, he had already consecrated the new collegiate church in his native
Castiglione Olona. A decade or so later, Masolino was painting for him the
delightful frescoes in the local baptistery and those in the family palace.[32]
For a prelate to concern himself with the restoration both of his Roman
seat and with that of his place of origin continued to seem a reasonable
policy. We find Nicholas taking charge of certain restorations in Bologna
where he had attended the university, Pius rebuilding his native town of
Corsignano as Pienza and Sixtus adding to the Duomo at Savona a mortuary
chapel for the della Rovere family to which he belonged.

The third basilica to receive Martin's attentions, S. Maria Maggiore, was,
as we have already seen, particularly cherished by his own family, the Colonnas. For one of their four chapels in the basilica, Martin asked Cardinal
Branda's favorite artist, Masolino da Panicale, to paint an altarpiece in which
the pope should himself appear in the guise of Pope Liberius tracing the
floor plan in the miraculous snow.[33] (figure 7) Masolino was probably
assisted by the young Masaccio who seems to be responsible for the figures
of the Baptist and St. Jerome.[34] (figure 8) We have already observed that

[30] G. Vasari, *Le vite de' più eccellenti pittori* etc., ed. Milanesi, 1878, III, p. 7.
[31] Vienna, Kunsthistorisches Museum. B. Degenhart, *op. cit.*, p. 81 and frontispiece.
[32] For Branda da Castiglione's patronage of Masolino cf. p. 51 in the article by U.
Procacci cited in n. 7. See also P. Toesca, *Masolino a Castiglione Olona*, Milan, 1946.
[33] *Vite, ed. cit.*, II, p. 294.
[34] Cf. n. 17 *supra*.

another panel of this altarpiece, in that case by Masolino, showed us the pope's patron saint, Martin of Tours, dressed in his namesake's cope. In Masaccio's panel we can detect a reference both to the church in which the *ancona* originally stood and to the pope's distinguished family connections. Instead of the simple reed cross customarily carried by the Baptist, we see here a column — that is, *colonna* — surmounted by a cross. Just such a cross-crowned column had been a familiar landmark in the piazza outside the church since the beginning of the eleventh century.[35]

It was clearly impossible for Martin to forget his noble kinsmen even when he acceded to the throne of St. Peter. He made his nephew Prospero a cardinal at the age of twenty-two and Prospero immediately set about putting into practise his uncle's admonitions in regard to titular churches and their adjacent palaces. Prospero's palace has since been replaced by a later structure. It probably looked a good deal like the only remaining palace of the period, that of the Cardinal Domenico Capranica, which is more or less faithfully echoed in Angelico's *Preaching of St. Stephen*.[36]. But we know something about the Colonna garden from a brief description written by that ardent antiquarian, Cyriacus of Ancona, in 1432. Once one starts digging in the soil of Rome one is bound to find something of interest below the surface. Somewhere on the hill behind the palace, Cardinal Prospero found the famous marble copy of a late Hellenistic bronze *Marsyas,* usually called the "Belvedere torso" because it has been in the Vatican collections since the 1520's. (figure 9). Until modern times, the marble was identified as an image of the virtuous Hercules. The presence of this striking sculpture in the cardinal's garden marks the beginning of the fashion of assembling collections of ancient marbles both within and without the palces of Rome, and, consequently, sparks the trend which led to the modern museum.[37] (figure 10)

The torso certainly aroused the enthusiasm of the young Prospero Colonna for antiquity. He was later dubbed the "new Mecaenas" of his age and we are gratified to find him restoring ancient buildings just as his uncle had restored the Early Christian basilicas and the Pantheon. A few years later another notable Roman palace garden, which was designed by Alberti for the Cardinal Pietro Barbo, was even described as "a haunt of the dryads."[38] We soon hear of a supper party in the palace when the cardinal's fabulous collection of ancient gems was consulted to settle points of Latin orthography and pagan myth.

[35] M. Armellini, *op. cit.,* I, p. 282.

[36] L. Callari, *I palazzi di Roma,* Rome, 1944, p. 117.

[37] C. Nolan Spencer, *The Belvedere Torso,* typescript of Master's thesis in the Smith College Library, 1952, p. 4. See also P. P. Bober, *Drawings after the Antique by Amico Aspertini,* London, 1957, p. 19, n. 1 and p. 34. See also C. Huelsen, *Römische Antikegärten,* Heidelberg, 1917.

[38] Cf. R. Weiss, *op. cit.,* p. 40. Other references to Cardinal Barbo's humanist interests occur throughout this pamphlet. For the supposition that Alberti was the architect of the Palazzo Venezia cf. L. Callari, *op. cit.,* p. 129 ff.

For it is the renewed enthusiasm for ancient art which marks the decade of Martin's papacy. He probably cared very little for it himself except as a symbol of Rome's glory, just as he seems to have cared very little for books. Martin left almost the whole papal library at Avignon whence it was brought back by Eugenius and eventually established by Sixtus as a major feature of the Vatican. By that time the library contained over 2,500 Greek and Latin codices, many of which had been procured by Nicholas. The humanist Platina was appointed its librarian and many celebrated miniaturists of the day were adding to its treasures.[39]

But whether or not Martin cared for literature either ancient or modern, he had to have secretaries to write his letters and his bulls. They had to be able to write the beautiful cursive hand called "cancelleresca"; and they had to be able to compose sentences in flawless Petrarchian Latin.[40]

The eldest of Martin's distinguished secretaries was Poggio Bracciolini, who employed his leisure hours in writing an account of the antiquities of Rome and in forming a collection of his own, often asking the great Florentine sculptor Donatello for advice on his purchases.[41]

The appearance of a younger secretary of possibly greater importance, Leon Battista Alberti, is, fortunately, known to us through a self-portrait, since Alberti was not only a literary man and an antiquarian but was also an artist of major consequence, especially in the realm of architectural design.[42] (figure 11) Alberti was probably in Rome by 1428 or 1429. He thus became acquainted with Masaccio shortly before the latter's death. Alberti obviously recognized that Masaccio's work was more original than that of any of the other painters employed by Martin or his cardinals since the precocious young Florentine is the only painter beside Giotto mentioned as worthy of praise in Alberti's treatise on painting.[43] This epoch-making book was written in the mid-1430's to give a theoretical basis for the new style of art which had begun in Florence in the '20's. The Italian translation from the original Latin is dedicated to the great architect Filippo Brunelleschi who had worked out the geometrical system of perspective which was an essential element in the new painting and relief sculpture. Brunelleschi also seems to have been in Rome in the late '20s on one of those periodic journeys to study its ancient architecture and may have returned there at the beginning of the '30s. Ghiberti likewise probably came to Rome toward the end of Martin's reign. Donatello, and his companion, the architect and sculptor Michelozzo, were certainly in Rome in 1431 and 1432. They were then engaged on the Taber-

---

[39] E. Müntz, "La Bibliothèque du Vatican au XVe siècle," *Bibl. des écoles françaises d'Athènes et de Rome,* 1887, gives the history of the papal library during this period.

[40] D. Covi, "Lettering in Fifteenth Century Florentine Painting," *Art Bulletin,* XLV, 1963, pp. 1-19, with bibliography on the development of calligraphy.

[41] R. Krautheimer and T. Krautheimer-Hess, *op. cit.,* pp. 277 ff.

[42] For Alberti's life cf. G. Mancini, *Leon Battista Alberti,* Florence, 1911.

[43] L. B. Alberti, *On Painting,* trans. J. Spencer, London, 1956.

nacle of the Sacrament which Eugenius had ordered for St. Peter's. It is apparent from the relief of *The Entombment of Christ* at the top of this tabernacle that Donatello had followed Alberti's advice and had studied a Meleager sarcophagus then walled into a house at the foot of the Capitol, for the sculptor has clearly differentiated the limpness of the dead Christ from the animation of the living mourners around Him as Alberti said an artist should do. All these artists, with the exception of Michelozzo, are mentioned by Alberti with pride as his friends, and the friendship seems to date from his earliest days in Rome.[44]

Thus, between 1428 and 1432 — that is, during Martin's last years and the first years of Eugenius — Rome became the seed-bed from which the new phase of the Renaissance grew. Learned men began to study ancient art as well as literature, they began to associate with modern artists who seemed to them worthy of a place beside those sculptors and painters whom Pliny had recorded as being so much admired in their own day, and who, through their work and by their very eminence, could confer upon their patrons that immortal fame which, from Petrarch's time onward, was such a cherished objective of the men of the Renaissance. Because these humanists of the new type were scholars as well as connoisseurs they began to make a more systematic study of the Eternal City, and thus, eventually, to bring the science of archaeology into existence. Flavio Biondo, who dedicated to Martin's successor Eugenius his book on the monuments of pagan and Christian Rome, specifically states in the dedication that his book is more learned and reliable than the old-fashioned pilgrim's handbooks, appropriately entitled "The Marvels of Rome" because of the improbabilities which they relate. By 1432, Alberti was already at work on a large scale map with an accompanying description of Rome. Many years later, he was chosen as the appropriate guide to take the young Lorenzo de' Medici to see the sights of Rome when he came to congratulate Sixtus on his accession. Alberti's map has disappeared. It has been gussed that it is at least reflected in a drawing now in Mantua.[45] Whether or not this is true, it is certainly easier to find one's way about in the Mantuan view of Rome than in such a jumbled image as that by the Sienese Taddeo di Bartolo at the end of the fourteenth century.[46] And, naturally, Alberti's map led to the precise topographical studies of later centuries, made not only in Rome but elsewhere, and are, of course, related to the whole development of cartography which came with the voyages of discovery of the fifteenth century.

[44] Cf. R. Krautheimer and T. Krautheimer-Hess, *op. cit.*, pp. 315 ff. for the friendship of Alberti and these Florentine artists in Rome at this time. It is, of course, possible, that Donatello saw the significance of the Meleager relief himself and called Alberti's attention to it.

[45] G. Mancini, *op. cit.*, p. 290.

[46] Fresco in the Palazzo Communale, Siena. A. Muñoz, *op. cit.*, p. 3.

[47] V. Moschini, *Disegni di Jacopo Bellini*, Bergamo, 1943, p. 44. I am indebted to Phyllis W. Lehmann for this observation.

The effect on the artists who came to Rome was of no less importance than that on the papal secretaries. Gentile da Fabriano died in 1428, Masaccio in 1429, so that we cannot estimate their reactions, but Gentile's assistant, the Venetian Jacopo Bellini made drawings of the antiquities which he saw and worked them up in his famous "Sketch Book" which was still regarded by his sons as a valuable heirloom at the beginning of the next century. For instance, the *Hermaphrodite* which was in the Sassi palace in the sixteenth century was probably already above the ground in the 1420s, for a derivative of the figure stands just over the door at the right in Jacopo's drawing of the Story of Hannibal.[47] Masaccio's companion, Masolino, did not abandon his earlier graceful and joyous style in his post-Roman frescoes at Castiglione Olona, but he had made a drawing of some fragmentary torso which he used for the figure of the catechumen who is pulling off his shirt in preparation for his baptism. (figure 12) It may even have been the Cardinal Prospero's famous find.

Pisanello, who followed Gentile at the Lateran, changed his style of painting very little in his post-Roman years. It is amusing to see his translations of figures from Roman sarcophagi into a pure late Gothic idiom, in drawings which were being made at the very moment when Ghiberti was using the same sources for the much more classicizing figures of his second door, like the *Samson* from the frame. But in his sculpture, Pisanello utilized his Roman experience in quite a different way. At his death in 1455, the prelate Carlo de' Medici acquired a number of ancient silver coins and medals from the artist's estate. Pisanello so loved these small Roman treasures, that five years after his return from Rome, he made for the Emperor John Palaeologus of Byzantium, then attending the Congress of the Eastern and Western Churches at Ferrara, the handsome medal with the imperial portrait on the obverse and a scene of the emperor's prayer at the cross-roads on the reverse.[48] It was the first in the long series of Renaissance portrait medals which have preserved for us the appearance of the famous men and women of the time. With special pleasure we may note that Paul II, who had meanwhile acquired Pisanello's collection from Carlo de' Medici, thought the artist's modern medals such worthy successors to the ancient coins they both loved, that he caused impressions of them to be made on the gilded lead tiles of the church of S. Marco which adjoined his palace.[49]

The impact of the sculpture and architecture of ancient Rome on Donatello, Brunelleschi, Ghiberti and Michelozzo is too well known for comment, and throughout the century it is possible to idenitfy numerous quotations in the work of various visiting artists. Less attention has been paid to the in-

[48] G. F. Hill, *Pisanello*, London, 1905, pp. 45 ff.

[49] J. Stevenson, "Notes sur les tuiles de plomb de la Basilique de St. Marc ornées des armoires de Paul II et des médaillons de la Renaissance," *Mélanges d'archéologie et d'histoires*, VIII, 1888, pp. 455-62 and Pls. 5-6.

terest which these visitors took in the remnants of Roman painting, because so much of what they saw has since been lost.   In fact, however, the resemblance between Castagno's frescoes done about 1450 for the Villa Pandolfini near Florence and a room in a villa discovered near Pompeii at the beginning of the present century, suggests that Andrea saw in Rome similar wall-paintings which have since disappeared, since he adopts a similar spatial device.   Furthermore, Castagno's wall is made up of panels of simulated porphyry and serpentine such as are often represented in ancient painting where they imitate the sumptuous real walls of palaces and public buildings.[50]

Another instance comes from the Sienese Francesco di Giorgio's cassone panel now in the Louvre.   Francesco visited Rome in 1480 and probably saw the vault of one of the rooms in Nero's Golden House known to us today only from such drawings as those in the Codex Escurialensis and the sketch book of Francisco d'Hollanda.   The highly improbable pose of Europa as she rides on the white bull is remarkably like that of the figures which the Roman painter Fabullus perched on the back of his fantastic monsters in the four corners of the vault of Nero's Golden House.[51] (figure 13)

Thus, the lure of Rome, both pagan and Christian, plus the continued lack of local competition made a Roman journey seem a necessity to generations of artists, from Raphael in the sixteenth century to Rubens in the seventeenth, Fragonard in the eighteenth, Ingres in the nineteenth, and even to Picasso in our own day.   Perhaps Martin V would have been somewhat surprised to think that he had been responsible for so much, but, on the other hand, he might have thought it only reasonable that we should give him his share of credit, for his coins bear the legend "the rebuilder of desolate Rome" and his tomb the inscription "the felicity of his times."[52] (figure 14) And, curiously, since the Holy Year of 1950, it has become the custom to throw coins into the open crypt in which his tomb has now been placed in front of the tabernacle at the end of the nave of the Lateran, as if in unconscious gratitude for his having made possible for everyone a Rome to which one can return.

---

[50] Cf. M. Salmi, "Gli affreschi di Andrea del Castagno ritrovati," *Bolletino d'arte,* 1950, pp. 295-308 and A. Maiuri, *La villa dei misteri,* Rome, 1947 and examples in G. Rizzo, *La pittura ellenistico-romano,* Milan, 1929. I am indebted to Mrs. Lehmann for this observation as well.

[51] A. Weller, *Francesco di Giorgio,* Chicago, 1943, p. 10 and p. 120; *Codex Escurialensis, ed. cit.,* f. 6; G. Rizzo, op. cit., Pl. 29.

LIST OF ILLUSTRATIONS

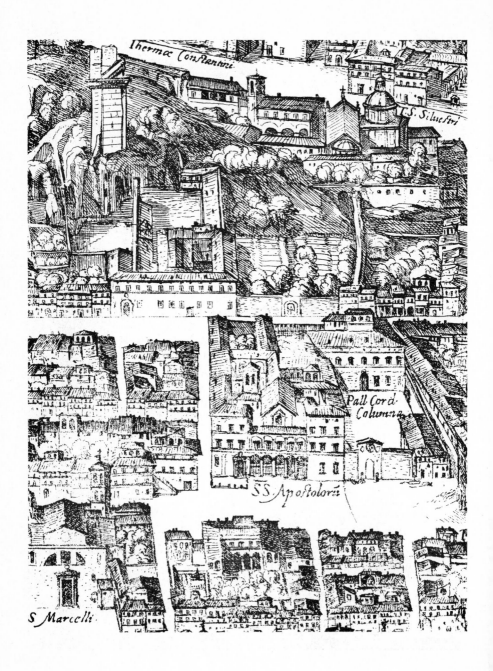

THE END OF THE RENAISSANCE IN ITALY
1530 - 1559

MAX SALVADORI

Professor of History

Smith College

ON PERIODIZING

"Periodizing," to use an ugly word, is simply a tool for helping our limited faculty to grasp the wide range of man's history. It has often been an obsession, especially for the hybrid intellectuals and pseudo-intellectuals rather equivocally described as philosophers of history. Its role must not be underestimated, however: the wonderful historical syntheses fascinating to uncritical minds, some of which, with tragic results, have been powerful spurs to action, are usually just unsubstantiated speculations about periods — not about facts. When dealing with periods minds float unhindered, far from the reaches of scientific thought and scientific method. Like all classifications of historical material, periodizing goes beyond a simple ordering of events with the aid of elementary rules of formal logic. It involves weighing and screening the data, i.e., making use of value judgments; it requires the fullest use of ability to associate and abstract; it cannot be dissociated from subjectivity. Periodizing implies — whether consciously, as is desirable, or subconsciously — the formulation of the criteria it is founded on. Most historians will maintain that all they have done has been to observe, that the criteria used are implicit in the historical process and inherent in the data; that their periodizing simply mirrors historical reality. The more sincere they are in this assertion, the more they delude themselves and will, unwittingly, deceive readers and listeners. Any criterion the historian adopts is only in part the outcome of observation: mostly it is the result of inventiveness, in plain words it is the fruit of imagination, guided by ideals and visions, by biases and prejudices — hence by emotion more than reason. Certainty is lacking: there is only the hope that what the mind has produced corresponds to the historical reality, that subjective and objective history are one.

The Ancients had their golden, silver, bronze and iron ages of which poets sang. Imaginative Moderns have invented the Four Ages, the Three and Eight Stages of human development somewhere or everywhere, ebbs and flows, Divine Revelation through chosen ancient and modern nations, primitive communism to ultimate communism through oriental agrarianism and western feudalism and capitalism, divine and heroic and human stages in the development of the mind, revised later (without plagiarism, I assume) in theological and metaphysical and positive phases. It is enough to compare the conflicting and incompatible periods of equally competent modern thinkers, to become fully aware of the subjective and usually illusory character of periodizing. Vicoan, Hegelian, Comtian, Marxian, Toynbean ordering of events are all purely hypotheses. These can make for wonderful writing, but not soundness. The basis rule that Mill stressed concerning correct thinking applies to any kind of periodizing: an element of doubt as to its validity must always be preserved.

Except as a creation of the mind, there is no such thing as the Renaissance (or the Age of Faith which presumably preceded it, and whatever Age followed it — of the Counter-Reformation, of Despotism, of Capitalism, of Foreign Domination, according to the writer's bias). But because common elements persisted through the generations in the form of concepts and values, attitudes and interests, institutions and customs; because of the persistence of certain webs of relationships; and because of similar and related events — the historian can write about the Renaissance. This he may do provided he remains aware that he is using a product of his own mind to cover a myriad situations, events and individuals; provided he realizes there is no scientific proof that his mind mirrors the historical reality correctly; and if he avoids the common error of shifting reality from the concrete (the single happening) to the abstract (the general term embracing the myriad happenings).

TIME SPAN OF THE ITALIAN RENAISSANCE

Periodizing is usually done in terms of a single date and a single event: 338 BC, 1776, the deposition of Romulus Augustulus, the capture of Constantinople. But seldom does something happen that radically and suddenly modifies a situation. In the life of the communities involved, there was not so much difference between 339 and 338 B.C, between 1775 and 1777; not many contemporaries were aware of what happened to young Augustulus, and those who were did not — so far as we know — attach much importance to it; and Constantinople had for so long been on the verge of capture that its fall was just one episode among many. The historical landscape of a few consecutive years is not likely to be more varied than a few consecutive miles of physical landscape before or after the branching off of a road leading in another direction. Any debunker can shrug his shoulders and point out that as 1559 is little or no different from 1557 and 1558, from 1560 and 1561, it cannot mark the end of a period; and if there is no end, presumably there is no beginning — in short there is no period, no Italian Renaissance. Modern debunker and ancient sophist can agree in holding that in the chain of historical events no one link is different from any other.

To observe the change in an historical landscape, it is best to take into account not a single event and a single date, but what happens during a whole generation, and the change that we can document in the way of life of that generation. A generation is not just people who have reached maturity at approximately the same time and have been for the usual score and a half years or so the active element in the national community. Generations include people who may have been born within a fairly wide range of years, but who have something in common because they have gone through the same or similar experience, have shared similar values, have faced similar problems (that they may have reacted differently is secondary: there are generations characterized by great cohesion, others by bitter antagonisms). The Romans who witnessed the Goths' devastations of 409 and 410 may have been 15 or 45, but for the rest of their lives they were influenced by that experience: they were the generation of Alaric's Sack of Rome — and of St. Augustine. The break in Italy between earlier and later Middle Ages occurs at the time when the peninsular south became the Apulian duchy, and when elsewhere champions of secular and ecclesiastical power took up arms against each other. Those who lived through the events leading to the victories of Robert Guiscard in 1071 and 1072 to Canossa in 1077 belong to the same generation, whether born in 1030 or 1060.

Paying homage to the dictum of Comenius, man of God and great educator, that all things have their explanation in their beginnings, mention of the origins of the Italian Renaissance should be made so that the end be better understood. The conventional historical scheme is a simple one — and unless one is interested in trivial debunking there is no reason to dismiss it as wrong simply because others have considered it right. A new situation arose in Italy during the second half of the 11th century — or rather two situations, one in the South and the other, of longer duration, in the North. In both the peninsular and insular South the heavy swords of Norman knights ended Byzantine, Longobard and Saracen rule and ended too the autonomy of a few small but prosperous, and previously for a short time progressive, maritime communities. In the more secure and relatively more prosperous environment of a strong efficiently administered state, under the benevolent protection of capable, enlightened monarchs, activities of the mind flourished. The flourishing was limited and did not last long; but Palermo in Sicily, the capital of the united Kingdom for over a hundred years, was the first seat of the cultural revival later called the Renaissance. What Palermo had been in the 12th and 13th centuries with Norman Hautevilles and Swabian Hohenstaufens, Naples was briefly in the 14th century, particularly good under King Robert, a Capetian Anjou. But in despotic societies, however efficiently run, golden ages are rare islands in an ocean of torpor and stagnation. As a rule, despotism — ancient, medieval and modern, western, eastern and oriental — represses the creative mind to the point of suppression. The cultural revival in southern Italy, first in the kingdom of the two Sicilies, then in the kingdom of Naples, was just a flash — or rather a series of short-lived flashes.

What benevolent despotism did briefly and intermittently in the South, freedom did for a longer time in the north and center of Italy. Instead of flashes in the darkness there was daylight; achievements were correspondingly greater and more enduring. Again in the second half of the 11th century, the Church, strengthened by reforming zeal, clashed with the Empire exercising feeble authority over an Italian kingdom which embraced northern Italy (except the fast-growing Venetian republic) and Tuscany in central Italy. The clash meant governmental paralysis; it meant less authority for papal as well as for imperial representatives and agents — bishops and abbots, lords great and small. Urban communities of the kingdom of Italy, of which there were more than in any other European or Middle Eastern area of the same size, were often left to themselves, or could expel imperial and papal *vicari* without risk. Citizens took the business of government into their own hands; they established councils, assemblies and parliaments, elected their own officials. However limited and unevenly distributed, there was a measure of political liberty— not just as meaningless independence but, what really counts, as government by the citizens — with its train of factionalism, partisanship, bitter conflicts and deep tensions. That was the age of the *comuni*. While factions fought against each other and against feudatories ruling in the countryside, business people — craftsmen and merchants — attended to their businesses, economic activities expanded, standards of living rose. This was already happening in the 12th century.

Activites of the mind became freer more slowly than political and economic activities. For generations after political emancipation it remained dangerous to think differently, as knew Arnaldo da Brescia and Cecco d'Ascoli whose words were silenced by burning fires. There was not yet a Renaissance. But after the Great Interregnum annulled what remained of imperial authority, during the second half of the 13th century; still more (because the seat of power had been closer), when Avignon's Babylonian Captivity annulled papal authority early in the 14th century, *comuni* and *signorie* of the no longer functioning kingdom of Italy and papal state became more lax in enforcing comformity. Because there was a multitude of conflicting autonomous states, what a religious reformer, a political thinker, a man of letters with an independent mind, an artist pursuing his own vision, could not say, write or do in one state, he could in another — as very many did, from Dante to Michelangelo. What had been a desperately slow process since the middle of the 11th century acquired impetus three hundred years later: new ideas appeared, new values took root, new attitudes developed, new visions guided artists' work. It was not much; the emancipation of minds was only partial and was limited to a ridiculously small section of the ten or twelve million people then living in the Italian peninsula and the adjacent islands. The laboring masses, the bulk of the population, remained untouched by the new way of life even if they suffered under its impact.

But in relation to the times, in relation to what had been going on before during the long sad centuries of decline in the ancient Mediterranean world and during the bleak centuries of Western Middle Ages, in relation to what was then going on elsewhere in most of Europe, activities of the mind were freer: the Renaissance had come.

Hindsight tells us that the Renaissance had been announced by innumerable events; that there had been plenty of forerunners, all the way back to the 6th century of Boetius and Gregory Magnus. But the Italian Renaissance starts its short life in the generation that heaped scorn on Ludwig IV and Charles IV, that laughed at the hollow pretensions of emperors without empire. It was also a generation — and this was considerably more important — they laughed at the ministers of a church whose heads were enjoying a good time in Avignon in the palace provided by princely cadets of the French kings. Not many years had gone by since the time of the first and second Fredericks, held in awe even when opposed; since the age of Innocent III, of St. Francis, of the great theologians, of the new invention called the Inquisition and the bloody suppressions of Albigensians, Waldensians and other believers. The laughter was the index of a revolution — a revolution more important in terms of a different way of life than Sicilian Vespers of 1282, Venetian *serrata* of 1297, Roman *tribunato* of 1347, Florentine *tumulto* of 1378, more important than the organization of large banking enterprises in Florence, of merchants' cooperative ventures in Venice and Genoa, of textile mills in Milan. Most Italians were shocked. Thoughtful people worried about the future and, with Dante, regretted the good old times. But the Renaissance, which had had its forerunners in the architects and chroniclers of the 12th century, in the poets surrounding Frederick II in Palermo, in the writers of the *dolce stil nuovo,* in Giotto's O, got under way with the generation that read the *Decameron* and gave, to those willing to venture along new lines of thought, the possibility (of course a limited one) to do so.

The sack in Rome in 1527; the rapid consolidation of direct or indirect Castilian rule over the islands inherited from the Aragonese kings over Naples, over the most important states of Tuscany and Lombardy, over Liguria, over several smaller states; the nightmare of Turkish advance in central Europe and in the western Mediterranean, with the siege of Vienna in 1529, with raids all along the Italian coasts and even in north-eastern Italy: these were some of the major experiences — or crises — that molded the generation of 1530-1559. Of other and more important developments, Italians did not seem to be aware: except for a few, they did not realize that they were living at the end of an epoch, that their lives were being transformed not so much by what was happening in their own minds and consciences. As usual, no one is blinder to the implication of what occurs than those who are witnesses to the events, or even participants. Literate, responsible Italians realized, of course, that there were problems, difficulties, possibly a temporary eclipse.

Not even Guicciardini foresaw the change that three decades would bring about. Educated Italians were still convinced that the people inhabiting Europe's garden were also the mind and the soul (and the purse!) of Christian, i.e. Roman Catholic civilization. Venice had survived Europe's combined attack and seemed more powerful than before. Italians were much in evidence as influential people in foreign capitals from Lisbon to Edinburgh and Warsaw. But in reality the balance of power had shifted in favor of Transapline states; political influence in European affairs had lessened; wealth in the country as a whole had declined (probably few were aware of it, as there was little thinking about economics). Pride, however, was as great as ever — as shown by the arrogance of Venetian ambassadors, of those on the papal throne or close to it, of members of high-ranking families.

The mature literate Italian of 1530, belonging to the small national elite, had been born at the end of the 15th century or early in the 16th. In his childhood he had heard of Lorenzo de' Medici and of Ludovico Sforza; he had been exposed to teachers of Latin and Greek whose interests and approaches had little or nothing in common with those of confessors and preachers to whom polite lip-service was paid; if interested in intellectual things, as many were, he knew about Pico, Leonardo, Savonarola, Castiglione; he appreciated art and artists. Italians of 1530 had been born of parents whose Italy — mostly at peace for forty years before 1494 — had been dynamic and prosperous, parents who were citizens or subjects of states among which five ranked high in European politics: the Kingdom (there was no need to add "of Naples"), the Serenissima, St. Peter's Estate, the Milanese Duchy, the Florentine Republic. They had grown when Italy had become a happy hunting ground for the Four Horsemen, when French, Spaniards and Imperial Germans invaded from every side, when revolutions and conspiracies followed each other in quick succession. Rulers and courtiers, men of thought and men of action — concerned with what was happening nearby and with what could affect Italy in the immediate future — were little aware of the implications of oceanic explorations and of conquests in distant continents; they were even less aware of the implications of the ninety-five theses nailed on October 31, 1517, on the door of Wittenberg's Castle-Church.

Italian textbooks are unanimous in mentioning a date and an event as marking the end of the period with which we are concerned. The date is 1559 and the event is the peace of Cateau-Cambrésis, temporarily ending the Franco-Spanish duel which had lasted for nearly two generations. The peace is unimportant as far as the Renaissance is concerned but the date is worth keeping: by 1559 a series of events, big and small, had finally added up to a change in the climate in which the dynamic minority of the Italian nation lived.

Individuals were not basically different in 1559 from what they had been in 1530. Of course many of the distinguished and influential figures of

1530 were no longer alive; others who had achieved renown during those thirty years or so were also gone. Among statesmen, Paul III and Ercole II were dead (and the old pontiff Paul IV would close his eyes in 1559). The patriot Burlamacchi, better known to future generations than to his contemporaries, had followed to the grave his fellow Tuscan, the modest and great patriot of 1530, Ferrucci. Among the distinguished men of letters and of science, and the great artists, Ariosto, Guicciardini, Tartaglia and Correggio had died. Aretino's poisonous and ribald pen wrote no more. But many remained who were no less illustrious and whose achievements were in no way inferior. Alive and active in spite of their old age were two of the greatest artists, Buonarroti and Vecellio; among men of letters there were three whose writings had an enduring influence over succeeding generations — Vasari, Telesio, Cellini; there were many others of great literary worth, although forgotten by later generations, like Bandello. Among men of science was Cardano; among leaders of men in clerical garb were Morone and the future pope Ghislieri; and among leaders of men in armor, old Andrea Doria, energetic able Cosimo de' Medici, young Philibert of Savoy.

There was no lack of distinguished men in all fields of human endeavor in the first two generations that followed 1559. Some may be described as truly great. Tasso the poet, Veronese the painter, Palestrina the composer lived then. Among leaders of men were Alessandro Farnese, the able opponent of William the Silent, and Charles Emanuel of Savoy who planned (unsuccessfully) the destruction of France; there were also, collectively, the rulers of the Venetian republic. Among men of God were the Catholic saint Carlo Borromeo and the Reformer Faust Socini, with his kinsman Lelio the founder of modern Unitarianism. The court of Alfonso II of Este was no less brilliant than that of Alfonso I had been. There was as much sordid tragedy in the Medicis of the younger branch as there had been among Malatestas and Baglionis a hundred years earlier. With Bruno, Campanella, Sarpi, Galileo minds soared and the range of man's knowledge expanded. At the same time there was less violence, there were fewer wars, revolutions, plots and counter-plots; there was greater order in the Italian states and, we can safely assume, greater happiness in the Italian nation — or at least less disorder and less unhappiness.

The radical change between the prevailing climate of 1530 and that of the generation which followed in 1559 is better understood when keeping in mind what happened to some of the people mentioned above. One man mirroring the change, who lived it within himself, was Tasso. In his tormented soul lived both the Renaissance and what destroyed it. It has been said by those who favored the new climate (a legion at the end of the 16th century) that Tasso was responsible for his own tragic life. But was the fear that pursued him everywhere and deprived his mind of its balance, purely a product of his imagination? When Ariosto lived there were as many, possibly more, assassins lurking in dark alleyways, as in Tasso's time — ready to avenge those who the poet's pen had insulted; for Ariosto just as for Tasso, loss of favor could mean dire poverty. But these were secondary things. What the man or woman who has something to say needs most is the first of Roosevelt's Four Freedoms: freedom of expression. Ariosto, like Bembo, Aretino and so many of his contemporaries or near-contemporaries felt secure because whatever he wrote no torture chamber would break his bones. If a ruler, in imitation of the anti-Renaissance Paul II, had thrown him into a dungeon, the protests of the citizens of the republic of letters would have freed him. Tasso was afraid: since the 1550's too many fires had been lit in the squares of Italian cities to punish dissenters and non-conformists; too many people whose only crime had been to voice their own convictions languished in jails or were chained to a galley bench. Fearful and disturbed, Tasso who had written his great poem from his heart, wrote, without his heart, a revised version.

The tormented soul of Tasso symbolizes and summarizes the changing climate. He was one of the many who suffered when the age of the Counter-Reformation replaced the age of the Renaissance, when the secular arm obediently enforced orthodoxy and conformity. The two Socinis saved their lives by going into exile, and so did other believers like Ochino and Vigilio who could not recant because their faith was sincere and great. The statue of Bruno in Rome's Field of Flowers (Campo de' Fiori) stands on the spot where he was burnt at the stake: his crime [?] to put reason above non-reason. Campanella (a utopian communist) spent twenty-seven years in dungeons. The powerful republic of Venice, the one really independent state in Italy after 1559, was barely strong enough to protect the life of Sarpi, critic of that council of Trent whose edicts are being revised four hundred years later. And Galileo, harassed, arrested, put on trial in his old age, went through the humiliation of recanting. Neither Italy nor the Italians had changed radically between 1530, the year when after four centuries the Florentine commune died, never to revive, in 1559. It was the spiritual climate in which Italians lived that had changed. There had also been a change in the political milieu with Spanish viceroys and governors in five capitals and Spanish puppets occupying princely thrones, but this was just one factor influencing the spiritual atmosphere. There had been a change in the economic conditions, but not such as to have more than a negligible influence on the values, beliefs, and emotions that make history what it is. Spanish rule and the policy of mercantilism played their role, but the main responsibility lay in what the Italians did to themselves. In post-Renaissance Italy free enquiry was the enemy; to curb it, freedom of expression was abolished. Rigid conformity was enforced — by the state made subservient to the monolithic church reorganized in 1540-1564, by public opinion guided and coerced by cruel servants of blind deities, dogmatism, fanaticsim, intolerance.   Church and public opinion were Italian, not foreign.

WHAT HAD MADE FOR THE RENAISSANCE

Whenever we engage in the amusing and not so innocuous game of mapping out the periods in man's history, we first of all have to decide what makes for any given period. A series of similar events — of wars or revolutions, of city or factory building? A certain way of worshipping God or gods, or — in the absence of Revelation — the use of a secular conceptual framework? Ethics? Class structure? The relationship between men and their means of production? Dynasties? Political systems? There is an infinite variety of criteria for periodizing. Each criterion is the expression of a vision of man and society belonging to the historian; none is objectively implicit in the historical reality. What follows expresses a point of view based on the postulate that the degree of liberty enjoyed by the individual mind — inner liberty from dogmas and external liberty from censorship — is a main key to the rise and fall of human societies.

Works of art and the diffusion of books by Latin and Greek authors have been the conventional hallmark of the Italian Renaissance. We can see the works of art and we can read the books: they belong to the concrete data apprehended by our senses and transmitted into our consciousness. But they are only the surface: the essence of the Renaissance is represented by what went on in the minds and consciences of artists and of members of the learned community. The artists of the Renaissance expressed their inner selves to a greater degree than had happened before. To an already high level of craftsmanship had been added a large measure of creativity. One feels in their works life pulsing ardently, creative energy flowing. There were, as before, rules to be followed, conventions to be obeyed. Creativity was not entirely free; there were curbs and controls imposed not so much by censors acting on behalf of the state as by public opinion. But during about two hundred years, the public opinion that counted — of the small, educated, moneyed, politically influential elite — was more lenient than public opinion usually is, and the range within which the artist could give rein to his creative powers was greater than it had been previously. Among learned people (those — the humanists — who took special delight in becoming acquainted with the writings of the Ancients), there was often more than erudition. They were not mere glossarists interpreting the written word according to a rigid pattern set within narrow bounds. Their interpretation implied an active process of the mind, it involved the use of critical faculties. For the groups of humanists in both big and small cities, to know what Plato meant and to discuss it was of greater interest than to learn what he said. There was no longer mere memorizing and parroting of Aristotle and Cicero. In

Ficino's circle and in many others, in the academies then being formed, there were lively undogmatic discussions — and the birth of new ideas.

Creativity and criticism mean full use of the mind's liberty. This we are all endowed with but rarely use, minds being too often repressed and coerced by the built-in chains of their own dogmas and superstitions, or frightened into rigid conformity by what Toynbee calls the tyranny of custom — more oppressive than any tyrant. The active inner process in this period could not be described as a free way of thinking (free thought is an even rarer occurrence in man's experience than free expression): but it was at least a freer way of thinking than had existed during the seven hundred years Bruni — historian and humanist — assigns to the Middle Ages, and during the preceding centuries of slow decline of the ancient Mediterranean civilization. Moreover a way of thinking cannot set the tone in a society — as Renaissance thinking did — unless it is shared by many of those who form the audience to which writers and artists address themselves. Behind the works of art and the books which were the external manifestation of the Renaissance, there is the light coming from the freer minds of thousands who wrote, painted, sculpted and designed buildings; also the light coming from the freer minds of hundreds of thousands who helped in the diffusion of books, who read, discussed and taught, who commissioned and appreciated works of art.

Famous authors have written brilliant essays on the man of the Renaissance. Aesthetes, critics and historians have at times created an idealized figure — such as one finds in the photograph of a bust entitled The Renaissance Man by Clarence Kennedy, Professor Emeritus at Smith College, which appeared in a recent publication. As usual, abstractions which aim at synthesizing the reality by oversimplifying it, can be misleading. The Renaissance Man as a single type is as unreal as the Christian and the worker as prototypes of all Christians and workers, or Robinson Crusoe or homo oeconomicus, or any other abstraction covering a varied reality. Conventionally, one thinks of the Renaissance as typified by the brilliant group in whose center stood Lorenzo the Magnificent and which includes Poliziano, Pulci, Pico, Ficino, Landino, Toscanelli — by the Florence of Verrocchio, Polaiolo, Botticelli, Lippi, Ghirlandaio, Gozzoli, Michelozzi. But there were more than these, and their like, in the Renaissance.

Men of the Renaissance, too, were Sigismondo Malatesta, cruel and false, as well as gentle, sincere, Guidobaldo da Montefeltro. To the Renaissance belonged the skeptic philosopher Pomponazzi and the agnostic Bembo, also Savonarola and Vermigli, in whom burned different fires of religious zeal. Polished Poliziano and urbane Castiglione were distinguished Renaissance writers just as much as satirical Folengo and bawdy Aretino. Men of the Renaissance were those who believed in liberty, like Lampugnani, Capponi and their friends, who established the short-lived Milanese and Florentine republics of 1447 and 1494; Machiavelli, who lost faith in liberty and joined the too numerous ranks of advocates of tyranny as panacea for man's ills; tyrants and would-be tyrants, both benevolent and malevolent. Not only Beatrice and Isabella d'Este and Vittoria Colonna were women of the Renaissance, but also mannish Caterina Riario, heretical Giulia Gonzaga, the high-class courtesan Tullia d'Aragona, Giulia Farnese whose complaisant body led her family to the highest ecclesiastical and temporal positions. Columbus, who had overcome prejudice and took reason for guide when he sailed westward, Caboto and Verrazano who brought English and French ships to the shores of an unknown continent, they all were men of the Renaissance.

The Renaissance was richness and variety of experience. It was a greater possibility than obtains in most societies at most tmes, to live a freer and therefore fuller, more productive life. The possibility was not less real for being the privilege of those who belonged to the Italian educated minority. As far as that minority was concerned there was less communalism — less control exercise formally or informally by the group over the individual. There was more individualism, and this was sufficient to make for a unique way of life. Richness and variety of experience made for great achievements — in fields material and spiritual; they made for progress and ultimately not Italy's progress alone. They also made for great tensions and considerable suffering: violence, cruelty, conflicts of all kinds, made the history of Italy from the early 14th century to the middle of the 16th a tragic one, and as much so for the passive masses as for the active participants in the drama. Unlike Christianity a thousand years before Boccaccio, unlike socialism four hundred years after Buonarroti, the Renaissance, as a way of life, never touched the masses. In this aspect it resembled the Hellenic golden age of ancient times, and the enlightenment and liberalism of the 18th and 19th centuries. With few exceptions — the most notable being urban Florentines and Romans — the masses continued to live their traditional communalistic life founded on total conformity and on supine obedience to authority, whether political or religious. They heaved a sigh of relief when the Age of the Counter-Reformation curbed minds and consciences and put an end to the exhausting effervescence of the educated minority.

The statement that a considerable measure of individual freedom was among the essential features of the Renaissance may seem strange to those who think along lines of conventional traditional history, concerned exclusively with political events. How could individuals be freer, even if this greater liberty was the privilege of the educated only, in the Italy of the *signori* (who in the process became princes), than they had been in the Italy of the *comuni* which had preceded it? Once again we find the evidence of what so often renders meaningless the best conceived plans: the logic of events — which man seems unable to grasp — differs considerably from the logic (or should it be called the pseudo-logic?) of the mind. Within conditions arising from the suicidal struggle between secular and ecclesiastical power in the age of Faith, an unusual development had occurred. Many minds had become emancipated from dogmas and superstititions; as rulers, monarchical or oligarchial, often shared in this emancipation, they did not use fully the power of the states they controlled with iron hands, in order to enforce intellectual conformity. If not directly, certainly through the activities of his son Caesar and of various henchmen, Alexander VI was a bloody tyrant; those who threatened his government or who were an obstacle to his political ambitions, were disposed of; but he did not care what people said and wrote as long as it did not directly concern his position as ruler. This had been true of Gian Galeazzo Visconti, of Alfonso d'Aragona, of Ludovico Sforza — as it had been of the Carraresi, the Scaligeri, the Polentas, the Malatestas, and countless other despots in states big and small. (It also explains the indifference towards the religious upheaval in Germany of Popes Leo, Clement and Paul for so many years after 1517: heresy did not bother them unduly until they became aware that it had political implications).

From the time when the medieval Inquisition entrusted to the secular arm the execution of Cecco d'Ascoli, until about two and a third centuries later, when the faction led by Caraffa triumphed in Rome and organized the more efficient modern Inquisition, men — and sometimes women — were suppressed in Italy for what they did, rarely for what they said or wrote. Accusations of sorcery still brought savage repression, but this was a special case. As a rule political opposition was a crime, not intellectual deviation. If Hus had lived in Italy, the widely-diffused religious indifference of the political and intellectual elite would have protected him. Savonarola was burnt at the stake in Florence's Piazza della Signoria: like Joan of Arc two generations earlier he had been condemned as a heretic, (which neither of them was, as proved by later rehabilitation in one case and current efforts at rehabilitation in the other); even more than Joan he was executed for political deeds. Political reasons induced Alexander VI to authorize his trial; for political reasons the Florentine Medici crowd rejoiced at his death, which was lamented by the republican minority. Neither the Pope nor the Medicis cared about Savonarola's theological position.

As in so many other cases in the history of mankind, the multiplicity of centers of political power helped to maintain that climate of relative freedom of expression without which, sooner or later, freedom of the mind atrophies and creativity weakens. What Cangrande and Guido Novello had done for Dante at the end of the age of Faith, what Frederick II of Prussia and Catherine II of Russia were to do one day for Voltaire, *signori* and princes did for countless writers and artists. The Venetian oligarchy was often willing to give shelter to those whose views led them into trouble in Rome; fugitives from Florence were welcome in Siena, forty miles away; Gonzagas and Estes gave protection and subsidies to those whose life and liberty were threatened in the lands of their respective opponents, Sforzas and Medicis.

The climate of Renaissance can be summarized in the humanists' slogan *ubi spiritus ibi libertas*. The freer use of the mind is the essence of the Renaissance; the chief characteristic of the times was a freer way of life than had been possible in the ages of Faith (although part of the time this had been also the age of the *comuni*) and of the Counter-Reformation. In the main areas into which Italy was divided there was Renaissance in the measure that expression was free, more in Rome than in Sicily, more in Florence than in Naples; the Renaissance lasted longer in Venice because — even after 1559 — there was still a freedom of expression which by then had disappeared elsewhere. The Renaissance did not die suddenly. Neither had it come suddenly: it had been prepared by centuries of erosion of the powers entrusted with the control of society. It had been born from the political disintegration of the Italian nation and its division into a multiplicity of warring but self-government communities, the result of the long-drawn-out civil war between Empire and Papacy. As was to happen later during the short period of liberal ascendancy in the nations of the West, the freer way of life had been accompanied by mounting tensions and conflicts. Their cumulative effect ended the Renaissance, in Milan earlier than in Rome, in Florence earlier than in Venice.

In times like the present when communalism is again in the ascendance, people come to look with more and more distaste at the conditions which made the Renaissance possible. In terms of their effect on the lives of the people, these conditions can be summarized with the word tension. With their suffering the masses paid for the achievements of the educated minority of their fellow-citizens. Whatever the ultimate evaluation in terms of good and evil, among the achievements humanism remains the main lasting feature. As already noted, to see in humanism mere erudition is a fallacy. It was the application of critical thought to the astounding crop of ideas formulated by ancient thinkers. Through humanism, ideas which had become part of the dead world revived. The revival that gave its name to the Renaissance was a revival of the mind and not just of interest in a restricted number of literary works. However limitedly, humanism had implied the priority of critical reason and therefore of reasonableness over dogmatism, rational or arational. It implied the tolerance described at the end of the 17th century in English-speaking Protestant nations as latitudinarianism, when practiced in that field of religion which had been for too many centuries the seat of intolerance and fanaticism, and hence cruelty. Humanism implied greater concern for the individual than for the group, and this was to be strongly resented later by all communalists postulating the priority of the religious congregation, the Church or any Church, or of the political community, the state. The Renaissance came and went. Frightened into subservience to anti-Renaissance forces, the educated minority which had produced the Renaissance came to lose interest. Humanism, however, survived in Italy, not as a school of thought but as an attitude towards human beings which has since remained widely diffused in the Italian nation. Fortunately for mankind it migrated north of the Alps, there to become the source of whatever good has existed in modern Western civilization: toleration, reasonableness, respect for the individual, humanitarianism.

THE POST-RENAISSANCE CLIMATE

Will Durant, acting as the devil's advocate, wrote in *The Renaissance* as follows on the period after 1559: "The Spanish hegemony was a boon to Italy. It put an end to the wars of the Italian states. . . . It gave the people continuity of political power. . . . It quieted the fierce individualism of the Renaissance. . . . Those who craved order accepted the subjugation with relief." And the 19th century historian and statesman, Balbo (a leader of the short-lived Guelf movement of 1846-49 and for a few months prime minister of Sardinia) commented as follows on Italy's age of the Counter-Reformation: "If that can be called happiness which gives to the people peace without activity; to nobles rank without power; to princes undisturbed authority within their states without independence; to writers and artists innumerable occasions for writing, painting, making statues, and erecting edifices with the applause of contemporaries. . .; to the nation ease without dignity and facilities for sinking tranquility into corruption. . . then no period of her history was so happy for Italy as the one hundred and forty years which followed the peace [of Cateau-Cambrésis, in 1559]. Invasions ceased. . . internal struggles ceased. . . popular revolutions ceased. Italians enjoyed life, indulged in the sweets of leisure, of vice, of contented lust. . . ."

Of course not all Italians enjoyed life. As is usual, Balbo identifies the part with the whole; but it was for the overwhelming majority, even if life was not enjoyed by Carnesecchi, Paleario, Bruno, burnt at the stake respectively in 1567, 1570, 1600, and hundreds of others who shared the same tragic end. Besides Campanella, Sarpi, and Galileo when under arrest or the threat of arrest, others who did not enjoy life were the scientists Fallopio and Cardan, beautiful and intelligent Giulia Gonzaga, or those who wandered as exiles in foreign lands. Statistically they were few, of course — at least in relation to the contented millions. Most Italians rejoiced in the change, of which they were well aware. There had been too many conflicts, too many wars, too much suffering. Most wanted peace above everything else. Peace and security. Peace there was, even if security proved to be purely a delusion. Not many Italians, even among the most sophisticated, ever considered what that kind of peace would do to the Italian nation; and those who did, found it unobjectionable. Spain enforced peace among states: satellites, as all were except for the Serenissima, were not allowed to fight each other even if at times they were allowed to fight on their own against outsiders (as was the case of Piedmont ruled by the Savoys). More important than the peace between states was the peace prevailing internally, achieved through severe enforcement of rigid conformity in all fields. Those whose *fiat* was the church's will dictated the rules of conformity; obediently the state enforced them. Under the new conditions intellectual life lost its effervescence. Few cared about it, and those few found no response among the many. Except for the intervention of the Venetian government on behalf of Sarpi, and a few other cases, there was no commotion, no protest when dissenters were arrested and tried, as had happened instead in 1467 when Paul II disbanded the Roman Academy and jailed Platina and Pomponio Leto. Cosimo de' Medici handed over Carnesecchi to the Inquisition, Mocenigo handed over Bruno. There was a lag between the decline in intellectual activities and the decline in economic activities. But not much. There had been some economic recovery in 1559 and there seemed to be no reason to be unduly pessimistic about the Italian economy in the years immediately following. However, by the end of the 16th century Italy was considerably poorer than at the beginning and the decline was to continue. Stagnation had set in, and would last until the accidents of European wars opened the country in the 18th century to beneficent political and intellectual foreign influences, under whose impact a slow re-awakening took place.

THE DEATH OF POLITICAL LIBERTY

Contemporaries knew that the fall of the republic of Florence in 1530 was a landmark. Those who lamented it, in Florence and elsewhere, were a minority: most of them hoped against hope — as usual in similar situations — that it would be a temporary eclipse, as it had been in 1347, and again before 1494, and in 1512. They hoped that one day there would be a revival of republican liberties. But these had become meaningless words for most citizens, who preferred to be contented subjects; they had become objects of derision for sophisticated intellectuals. The republic was gone forever and with it a way of life. Florence had been a self-governing community since early in the 12th century; it had later become a sovereign state even if nominally part of a non-existent empire. By the end of the 13th century it had become the leading Tuscan city-state. All through the Renaissance it had been one of the five major Italian powers. The smallest in area and population, it had ranked at times first, at times second, economically. It had outranked all others in the richness of its intellectual life. In the history of mankind, among local communities only Athens compares with Florence for its achievements. No one should remain unmoved when reflecting on the astounding ten generations or so of Florentine and Athenian glory.

A semi-democratic regime in the 12th century — democratic for the times — had been replaced by an oligarchic one and this by a presidential one. Since the first half of the 14th century republicanism and all it implied of government by discussion, of free elections of officials, of internal liberties, was rejected by an increasing number of Florentines who were tired of un-certainty, factionalism, party conflicts, dissensions. An increasing number wanted internal peace and shared the common illusion that strong centralized irresponsible power guarantees peace, and with it prosperity and progress. The presidential republic of Cosimo de' Medici was becoming a monarchy under his grandson Lorenzo. However, monarchism, wanted by minority sections of the upper and middle classes and by a majority of the masses in the capital and in the outlying territory, had its opponents. Republicanism had its loyal adherents, and in spite of monarchist tendencies among the masses and oligarchic tendencies among the upper classes, Florence was still the center of Italian republicanism. The French invasion of 1494 helped the republican minority to seize power. The Medicis left but their supporters remained, and in 1512 they were again in control of the state. On behalf of the heads of the family engrossed in the temporal affairs of the church, rela-tives governed Florence. Taking advantage of the political weakness of the Medici pope besieged in Rome's Castel Sant'Angelo, the republicans triumphed for the last time in 1527.

Spanish-imperial troops had achieved numerous successes in 1525-29; the French and their Italian allies had been defeated; Charles V, wise enough not to overreach himself in victory, offered peace terms to Clement VII. Terms agreed on in Barcelona by representatives of Emperor and Pope were the basis for negotiations between the two in Bologna in the autumn of 1529. Above everything else, Clement VII wanted the re-establishment of Medici rule in Florence. The emperor consented (and in exchange was crowned with the Italian royal crown and the imperial crown in Bologna's cathedral). In December a papal-imperial army besieged Florence. The republicans, counting on French help, decided on resistance. Besides the defenders (little more than ten thousand of them on the city walls, strengthened under the supervision of Buonarroti), a small army of three thousand volunteers was raised to harass the besiegers in the countryside. It was defeated early in August 1530 by superior forces. Baglioni, whom the republican government had appointed commander-in-chief, betrayed his trust and opened the gates to the enemy. On August 12th the republic came to an end. Those re-publican leaders who did not immediately recant or escape, were executed. They had played the role Demosthenes and Leosthenes played in Hellas eighteen and a half centuries earlier, and Cicero and Brutus in Rome nearly sixteen centuries earlier. Ferrucci, Carducci, Capponi, Girolami and the other republicans had been overwhelmed by the wave of the future which prom-ised — as it had once promised Greeks and Romans, as it promises today under different labels — peace, prosperity, and, for those who care, even progress, all under despotism. Amorgos put the seal on Cheronaea, and Philippi on Pharsalus: the fall of Florence confirmed the triumph of forces which had been gathering strength in Italy during the previous decades. In ancient times what Philip of Macedonia and Caesar had done became final with Antipater and the Second Triumvirate. In Florence their role was played by Duke Alexander on behalf of his uncle, Clement VII. No longer will the citizens of Florence govern themselves, their status will be that of subjects. The era of political liberty was over — to the contentment of most.

However, hope dies hard, and for several years attempts were still made to revive the past. Encouragement came from possibilities which seemingly resulted from conflicts among external powers. In 1529 peace had been signed between the two most powerful European rulers, the emperor and the king of France. Negotiations having been entrusted to two women of highest rank, it was called the Ladies' Peace. But another thirty years were to pass before it became a little more than a scrap of paper. There were direct wars between Spain and France, and indirect wars fought by satellites and by permanent or occasional allies. The direct wars, fought in Italy as elsewhere, were those of 1536-38, 1542-44, 1552-59. In 1557 the French made their last attempt of the 16th century to reconquer the southern peninsula Kingdom, which French princes had held from 1266 to 1434, for which Charles VIII had invaded Italy in 1494, and for which the French and Spaniards had started fighting in 1502. For their military operations in Italy the Spaniards had as a base the Kingdom and since 1535 the duchy of Milan, annexed temporarily in 1535, definitely in 1540. The French had allies: the duke of Ferrara, the republic of Siena, the exiles from all states governed by Spain or by Spanish puppets, at times the popes. The French kings and their allies had hoped that the Protestant revolt in Germany would weaken the hold of the emperor and king of Spain in Italy, but this did not happen. At sea a continuing war was being fought by most Italian states against the Turks, independently from their allegiance to either Spain or France, or lack of allegiance as was the case of Venice. Suleiman, his armies and his fleets, were continually present in the minds of Italians. The names of Barbarossa and Dragut were symbols of terror. Turkish raids, or fear of raids, emptied coastal areas and islands of their population. There was incessant talk of a crusade. Major engagements against the Turkish ships were fought off Prevesa in 1538 and off the coast of Ponza in 1552.

Minor episodes of the major Franco-Spanish conflict affected Italy. In 1536 the French occupied Savoy and Piedmont and kept them under their rule for 23 years; the duke and prince had no state of his own until the Spaniards compelled the French to make restitution to Emanuel Philibert of Savoy, who had distinguished himself in 1557 at St. Quentin, the last important battle of the Franco-Spanish wars. In 1548 France had invaded the marquisate of Saluzzo in north-western Italy. The same year Spanish troops occupied Piacenza which, with Parma, pope Paul III had made into an autonomous state for his son in 1545; for a long time previously it had been part of the duchy of Milan, now a valuable dependency of the Spanish crown (the treasury of the king of Spain received about as much from the duchy as from the whole of Spain). Spanish troops, still in 1548, also occupied Piombino, the capital of a small principality on the Tuscan coast since the 14th century. The dukes of Urbino and the grandson of Paul III waged war for the control of the duchy of Camerino in the barren mountains of central Italy. A successful war enabled Paul III to terminate the autonomy of Perugia. Eleven years later, in 1551, papal troops and their allies moved to the conquest of Mirandola. A war of succession for the Montferrat ended with the acquisition of the duchy by the Gonzagas of Mantua, protégés of Charles V.

With hopes raised by this continuing turmoil, conspiracies were plotted, insurrections occurred. Duke Alexander was assassinated in Florence in 1537: as had happened two generations before in the conspiracy against Lorenzo and Giuliano de' Medici, the populace turned against the conspirators. Another Medici, young Cosimo, became duke, and at Montemurlo the last battle of Florentine republicans was fought, and lost. In 1546 an influential citizen of Lucca, Burlamacchi, inspired by republican ideals (which then were the embodiment of the idea of liberty) and by Protestant faith, organized a well-planned conspiracy to seize power in Lucca, re-establish republican liberties elsewhere in Tuscany, create a federation of free commonwealths and introduce religious toleration. The conspiracy was discovered; Lucca surrendered Burlamacchi unwillingly to the emperor's representatives. He was executed. In 1547 a conspiracy led to the death in Piacenza of duke Pierluigi, son of Paul III; another conspiracy, in Genoa, failed to kill the Spanish puppet Andrea Doria; an insurrection led by Carracciolo, Sanseverino (Protestant sympathizers), and others broke out in Naples; the rumor had spread that the able Spanish viceroy Toledo was planning to introduce the Inquisition in the Kingdom. The two conspiracies failed in their goal, and the insurrection was crushed. A conspiracy organized by Sanseverino failed to lead to another insurrection in Naples in 1552. Because of the activities of the Inquisition, anti-papal rioting broke out in Rome when Paul IV died in the summer of 1559. When war had started once again between France and Spain, an insurrection ended the rule of the pro-Spanish faction in the republic of Siena; an army sent by the duke of Florence captured Siena in 1555. The surviving defenders withdrew to Montalcino, a fortified hilltop village. Siena was annexed to Florence in 1557. On July 31, 1559, Montalcino surrendered. After a long agony, republicanism — the spirit of political liberty — was finally quite dead.

After the surrender of Montalcino, there still were 'republics' in Italy, four of them; in none, however, was there republicanism, in none were citizens free, in none did the spirit of liberty breathe. Since centuries past, the highly educated and responsible Venetian ruling class had evolved the institutions of the most enduring efficient political system that ever existed: a well-organized and properly functioning closed oligarchy guaranteed to the state the stability and continuity which have always been the dream of most thinkers and the goal of most common people, which in open systems, democratic or oligarthic, are continually threatened by the changing emotions of the citizens, and in dictatorships, dynastic or other, are threatened by the whims of dictators and the problem of succession.   Within its despotic structure, Venice remained powerful enough to keep its independence, and for a while its prosperity.   It could even afford at times a measure of freedom of expression — less than there had been elsewhere in northern and central Italy in the heyday of the Renaissance (Venice had been the first state to introduce censorship of printed publications), more for about two generations after 1559.   Under the Dorias, Genoa was a republic in name only.   To prevent anything from happening that might antagonize powerful neighbors, and thus save its autonomy, Lucca restricted internal liberties to the point of suppression.   On top of Mount Titan, minuscule San Marino followed the current.

ECONOMIC SLUMBER

The absolutist wave of the future implied a promise of prosperity.   Lack of liberty made people unaware that economically they were going downhill. Duke Cosimo (grand-duke after 1569) could tell his subjects that they were better off than in republican times.   French and Spanish wars fought in Italy had brought about a good deal of destruction: fields untilled, cities devastated, shops closed, communications interrupted.   There had been famines and plague.   The worst period had been that of 1522-1530, but there had been others nearly as bad.   Moslem pirates (Turks, Levantines, North Africans from Barbary) had ravaged the coasts.   But recovery had at first been remarkably quick: in the Milanese after the disastrous events of 1515 and 1525, in Rome after the sack in the course of which the equivalent of hundreds of millions of dollars had been looted, in Florence after the siege. Mantua, Ferrara, Cremona, Pisa, Siena and countless others were far from being, at the middle of the 16th century, the dead cities they were to be in the 17th and 18th centuries.   In the 1530's and after, Venice was a great industrial and commercial center; agriculture and various crafts prospered in the Venetian possessions between the Adda and the Isonzo.   There had been little indication of economic decline in Genoa, whose bankers and merchants acted as treasurers, accountants and business executives generally for the Spanish administrations at home and abroad.   The economic dynamism inherited from previous generations was not yet dead in 1530.

However, the economic recovery did not last long.   Figures are available concerning the low level of industrial, commercial and agricultural activities late in the 16th century and early in the 17th; the closing down of textile mills in Milan, the state of disrepair of Venetian shipyards, the loss of trade in Lucca, the decline in the number of craftsmen and merchants, the lower agricultural production. A good deal has been written on the adverse effect of external factors on the Italian economy: the Portuguese monopoly of Asian and Indian Ocean trade, and the Spanish monopoly of American trade; the Turkish conquest of Egypt, the Turkish maritime control in the eastern Mediterranean and the Red Sea; the inflation caused by the influx of American silver, particularly after the beginning of the exploitation of the Potosi mines in 1545; the Protestant revolt which deprived the Roman church of as much as one-third of its income; the economic expansion of Atlantic nations. All this is correct but it is not sufficient to explain the rapid decline: monopolies were broken by Dutch, French and English; why not by Italians? Inflation affected all European economies. Contrary to the mercantilistic fallacy that one can become rich only to the extent that others become poor, the others' prosperity usually stimulates one's own. New markets could be found (an Englishman signed the first commercial treaty with Muscovy in 1553, why not an Italian?) Other factors were at work: what wars had failed to do was accomplished by the loss of dynamism — initiative, spirit of adventure, willingness to take risks — which followed in the wake of the triumph of despotism. The decline was also furthered by the short-sighted restrictive and protective policies of Italian states, both those governed by Spain and those which were more or less autonomous, and of Italian business interests, artisans' guilds, and merchants' and bankers' corporations.

At a time when sails were demonstrably more efficient than oars, Venetian, Genoese, Neapolitan and Tuscan shipyards went on building galleys which could not compete on the oceans with sailing ships. At a time when business communities, of Amsterdam and London particularly, were evolving new techniques of business organization (chartered companies, corporations, stock exchanges), Italian businessmen, who had been so inventive in the 14th and 15th centuries, kept to their traditional ways. When, in the wake of scientific discoveries, experimentation began in France, in Great Britain and elsewhere in western Europe, leading to technological inventions and more efficient modes of production, Italians remained absent. Italian traders kept to the Mediterranean, made smaller and poorer by Moslem piracy, while adventurers from the North Atlantic nations were trying, at their own personal risk and at the financial risk of their backers, to establish trade relations with non-European societies in all continents. No longer, among Italian businessmen, were there the economic adventurers that Bardis, Donatis, Dandolos, Acciaiuolis, had once been; there were no successors to Polos, Vivaldis, Zenos and Ca' da Mosto. To buy an estate and with it a title became more important for business people than to open a new branch or to expand an enterprise. Guild monopolies enforced by the state gave security to craftsmen and often ended by ruining the crafts in the long run. Taxation rose to the extent of destroying the taxable wealth, and was highly discriminatory. Everywhere in Italy, but particularly in the southern Kingdoms, the Papal States and Tuscany, the ecclesiastical mortmain reduced the circulation of capital considerably and depressed the economy. The 'conspicuous' consumption of the upper classes had a similar effect. There was an increase in the numbers of such non-productive groups of society as members of monastic orders and public officials. The Italian economic decline was due as much to changing values among the educated minority of the nation, as to changing economic conditions outside the peninsula.

DEATH OF THE FIRST FREEDOM

Changing values means what takes place in peoples' consciences and minds — the non-material aspect of life on which all culture is founded, from which derive the differences between civilizations and (as we are concerned with periods) between periods. Changing values were part of the radical transformation which in the course of one generation, between 1530 and 1559, occurred in the way of thinking of those who during the previous centuries had been the dynamic and creative minority of the Italian nation. The whole process is easily summarized: those who, for a variety of motives, were inspired by religious intolerance, increased in numbers and grew in determination. They achieved power in the Italian states and control over the Italian nation. They curbed, sometimes to the point of suppression, their main enemy, freedom of expression. Largely as the result of conviction, partly perhaps as the result of fear, conformity, dictated by the ecclesiastical power and enforced by the political power, triumphed. Intellectual activities declined, creativity withered.

This transformation was related to political changes, as effect and as cause. But the transformation itself is what matters above all — above politics, above economics. It was part of the religious upheaval which is the central theme of Western civilization in the 16th century. In some areas, in what were to become the progressive nations of modern and contemporary Europe, the religious upheaval led, at first on a small scale, later on a larger one, to the emancipation of consciences from the external authority of the clergy, then of minds from blindly accepted dogmas, then of citizens from monarchial and oligarchial rulers. A religious revolution was followed by an intellectual one and this by the political one. The religious upheaval made modern Western civilization what it was until recently, and launched it into the astonishing career which may be over for European nations but not yet for North American nations. In other parts of Europe, the upheaval meant greater subjugation of consciences to clerical power, of minds to dogmas, of citizens to the omnipotent state. Three generations after 1517 European nations were divided into two camps, progressive and traditional. The division will have its counterpart later wherever Europeans settled or established their control.

The Italian nation which for centuries had been the core of Western progressivism, because of the transformation of 1530-1559 ended up totally in the traditional camp.

During nearly two hundred years the range of intellectual nonconformity had widened considerably: it shrank rapidly after 1530 so that in three decades most of the ground that freedom of expressions and free enquiry had gained since the end of the age of Faith, was lost. Soon there was a generation which thought and acted as if there had never been the agnosticism, laicism and latitudinarianism of the Renaissance. It is true that, with variations according to place and time, it had been dangerous all through the Renaissance to be a believing Christian and not an orthodox Catholic. Statistical data are lacking, but the existence of underground communities of Cathari is known until the end of the 14th century, of clandestine communities of Waldensians and of heretical Franciscans all through that period. Execution was the punishment for heretics, as it was for those supposed to practice sorcery, witchcraft, occult arts, whenever the authorities could lay their hands on them. But unbelief was much less of a crime than unorthodox Christian belief — and more fruitful for the advancement of intellectual activities and the progress of the mind. Among the educated people in Italy there was no lack of Platonists and Aristotelians whose connection with Christianity was extremely remote; of empiricists, materialists, stoics, who paid (at times) lip service to Catholicism but were not believers. Reason mattered more than Revelation to humanists. There were free-thinkers teaching in the universities and participating in the discussions of the academies. The political elite had been composed largely of unbelievers. The change at the middle of the 16th century meant that any departure from orthodox belief in the direction of religious indifference, agnosticism and latitudinarianism, could not be tolerated any more than unorthodox Christian belief had even been tolerated. Institutionally, the change manifested itself through wider power given to ecclesiastical and secular tribunals, establishment and enforcement of severe censorship, and rigid control over educational institutions.

The limited freedom of expression which had made the Renaissance was now the victim of the struggle of orthodox conformity against the new, dynamic Christian belief which since 1529 was known by the vague and general expression Protestantism. Already in the 1520's, a certain number of Italian intellectuals had been attracted by what they thought to be Luther's and Zwingli's positions. Others had formulated their own 'protestant' position. For a while Italian humanists were more aware of what was going on in Germany, and shortly after also in France, than the ecclesiastical hierarchy. In the 1530's the Reformation made numerous converts. In Italy Protestantism had its own characteristics and differed deeply from both Lutheranism and Calvinism (although Calvinism was embraced by a few thousand Waldensians who had survived persecution). Reforming ideas were developed and formulated by humanists whose outlook did not differ essentially from that of Erasmus and Thomas More, not by people whose minds belonged to the medieval Age of Faith. Most Italian Reformers were the spokesmen of a reasonable, even rational, approach to Christianity (as exemplified by Socinian unitarianism), and of freedom of conscience (as was the case, among the most influential, of Vermigli and Ochino). When compelled to look for safety in exile, Italian Reformers found friends among the Zwinglians more than among Lutherans and Calvinists.

Cathari, Waldensians, Poverelli, Fraticelli and other believers of the age of Faith had found their followers chiefly among the common people; 16th century Italian Protestantism was instead limited almost exclusively to the educated classes. It had two main centers, in each of which a foreigner played a dominant role. In Ferrara, the duchess Renée was the daughter of Louis XII of France; she had arrived in Italy with a retinue of friends, most of whom were inclined towards the new religious ideas, as she herself was; she was generous in aid and protection to the Reformers. In Naples Valdés, a high Spanish official, had secretly embraced Protestantism and was responsible for the conversion or near-conversion of many distinguished Italians (besides Vermigli and Ochino, also Carnesecchi, Mellio, Caracciolo, Sanseverino and the two ladies Vittorio Colonna and Giulia Gonzaga). Groups of convinced Reformers could be found in various cities of the duchy of Ferrara (the largest was in Modena), in the university cities of Padua and Bologna, in Lucca. Siena was the birthplace of Lelio and Fausto Socini. Waldensians in Piedmont and Poverelli in Calabria received encouragement from educated Protestants or near-Protestants. A group of Anabaptists was organized in Vicenza in 1550.

The Catholic hierarchy, largely composed of mundane and skeptical prelates, was slow to realize the importance of what was going on. There were also some sincere believers, who had been responsible, for instance, already in 1517 when no one in Italy had heard of Luther, for the organization of the Oratory of the Divine Love which aimed at reforming the church. To sincere Catholic believers had also been due the establishment of new severe monastic orders. When in the 1530's awareness spread to the implications of Lutheranism in Germany, of the growing number of Protestant converts in Italy, of the English secession, the Catholic reformers split into two groups: the moderates who wanted concessions enabling the Protestants to return to Catholicism, and the extremists or integralists who rejected all concessions, theological and administrative. Among the moderates (in Italian, *conciliatoristi*) were those with a humanist education who shared the humanists' approach to life and its problems: Contarini, Sadoleto, Bembo, Giberti, Morone. Their most illustrious foreign supporter was the Englishman Reginald Pole. Among the extremists (*rigoristi*) were the leader Caraffa, also Del Monte, Cervini, Ghislieri, and among the younger ones Peretti — respectively the future popes Paul IV, Julius III, Marcel II, Pius V, Sixtus V, all of whom reached the papal throne after having proved their worth as efficient inquisitors. The moderates wanted to do four centuries ago what many Protestants and liberal Catholics hope will be achieved through the efforts of the World Council of Churches and the Vatican Council in the second half of the twentieth century. The moderates tried, but after Contarini's failure to get hierarchical approval of an agreement discussed with Melanchton at the meeting of 1541 in Regensburg, they lost. The extremists were strengthened by the unyielding will and clear minds of the Spaniards Loyola (resident in Rome since 1537), Laynez and Salmerón. The Jesuit order, organized in 1534, received the papal blessing in 1540. The Jesuits were first and foremost educators: within two decades they controlled, directly or indirectly, all Italian educational institutions which were finally purged of skeptics, agnostics, dubious Catholics and non-Catholics. At the insistence of the Caraffa faction, the Roman Inquisition was established in 1542: trials began soon after and fires were lit in all Italy to suppress, along with heresy, freedom of conscience (the second of the Four Freedoms). In December 1945 the often postponed Catholic council opened in Trent — an alpine city, Italian in language, papal in obedience. Suspended in 1547, reconvened by Julius III in 1551-52, then again by Pius IV in 1562, the council ended in December 1563 with a solemn plenary session at which cardinals, archbishops, generals of monastic orders, and abbots gave their final approval to the *Professio Fidei Tridentina*. Theologians can discuss the religious aspects of the council. Intellectually and politically it made Catholicism what it has been until the current crisis, of which no one can foresee the outcome. It put the seal on the way of life of the European nations — from Portugal to Lithuania — and their offshoots in other continents, in which all heresy was extirpated. Italy was among them. Early in 1559, attempts made since 1520 to channel thought along severe orthodox lines reached their triumphant climax in *Index Auctorem et Librorum Prohibitorom*. Wherever the Inquisition and the Congregation of the Index held sway — soon everywhere in Italy — freedom of expression (the first of the Four Freedoms) ended.

With the events leading to the *Index* and to Montalcino, the Italian nation was at last free from what for most people is the heaviest burden, that which distresses them more than all else and fills them with anxiety, doubt, and awareness of their own inadequacy: liberty of minds and consciences, liberty of the citizens — spiritual and political liberty. There had been great achievements, there had been much suffering — more than most could endure. Only a few individuals still stood against the "wave of the future" — that eternal wave founded on the mirage of happiness, security and plenty in an orthodox authoritarian society admitting neither opposition nor deviation. "The Commentaries of Pius II" —wrote Miss Gabel in the book she published in 1959 — "depict an epoch of mounting crisis on many fronts." Where the Italian nation was concerned the crisis was for the most part over in 1559; and with it the Renaissance.

SUMMARY OUTLINE

1) Subjectivity of historical periods.   2) Remote and recent periodizing.
3) A justification and a warning.

TIME SPAN OF THE RENAISSANCE

4) A year is usually not a milestone.   5) Change is better measured in terms of generations.   6) The pre-Renaissance in the South.   7) Political liberty and rising prosperity in the North.   8) Slow emancipation of minds.   9) Boccaccio's generation.   10) Crises moulding the generation of 1530-1559. 11) The recent past.   12) Meaninglessness of Cateau-Cambrésis.   13) Little change in individuals.   14) Distinguished post-Renaissance individuals.   15) Tasso's inner conflict.   16) The post-Renaissance climate.

WHAT HAD MADE FOR THE RENAISSANCE

17) Variety of criteria for periodizing.   18) Minds creative and critical. 19) Liberty.   20) No single Renaissance type.   21) Variety of Renaissance types.   22) Tension and suffering.   23) Limited political freedom.   24) A latitudinarian attitude.   25) Multiplicity of despots weakens political despotism.   26) The climate of the Renaissance.   27) Humanism, the most valuable fruit of the Renaissance.

THE POST-RENAISSANCE CLIMATE

28) Devil's advocate.   29) Post-Renaissance contentment.

THE DEATH OF POLITICAL LIBERTY

30) Florence.   31) Resiliency of republicanism in Florence.   32) The end of the republic.   33) Continuing wars.   34) Other conflicts.   35) Unrest. 36) Republics without republicanism.

ECONOMIC SLUMBER

37) Temporary recovery.   38) The decline sets in.   39) Factors in the economic decline.

DEATH OF THE FIRST FREEDOM

40) Intellectual liberty, the enemy of the wave of the future.   41) Progressive and traditional West.   42) The elimination of unbelief.   43) The inroads of Protestantism.   44) Centers of Italian Protestantism.   45) The Catholic rebound.   46) *Index* and Montalcino.

SOME THEOLOGY ABOUT TYRANNY*

Guenter Lewy

Associate Professor of Government,

University of Massachusetts

Our generation, accustomed to thinking in secular categories, easily grows weary of the theological wrangling of earlier days. The old quarrels about predestination and free will have lost much of the ardor that once inspired passionate disputation, and the intricacy of grace makes most of us exclaim with Voltaire, "Who can understand its nature, its operations, the *sufficiency* which is not sufficient, and the *efficacy* which is ineffectual?"[1] And yet, at one time some of these doctrinal niceties were extremely important not only for the theologian but also for the political philosopher.

It is a commonplace to say that most political thinking during the Middle Ages and the Reformation period was wrapped up in the language of theology. But the actual interdependene of theology and political ideas during those centuries is perhaps even greater than is generally acknowledged. The question of the legitimacy of opposing unjust political authority, for example, seems closely linked to the theological paradox of theodicy — the eternal question *si Deus bonus, unde malum* — and to the problem of free will and predestination. Is evil in the world the result of man's own perversity or is it part of God's plan — punishment for man's sinful conduct? Are tyrannical rulers perverting an office of divine ordination or are they sent by God in retribution for man's depravity? Are tyrants personally responsible for their wicked deeds or are their wills enslaved by the original sin of Adam and driven to do evil by the divine decree of reprobation? It is the neglect of these doctrinal questions which often prevents the full understanding of certain seemingly political problems. Thus it is impossible to comprehend the emphatic insistence on non-resistance to temporal authority, no matter how wicked, on the part of St. Augustine, Luther and Calvin without taking into account their deterministic theology and their pessimistic view of the nature of man. On the other hand, John Milton's spirit of political activism, expressed in his vigorous defense of tyrannicide, is clearly related to his rationalistic interpretation of Christian dogma and his stress on human self-assertion in the relation between God and man.

One occasionally encounters the view that reliance on human effort and free will in the realm of theology hardly ever left any appreciable impact on political thinking, while, conversely, servitude before God is said to have

---

* A slightly different version of this article was published in German, in *Der Staat* II (1963), 197-211.
[1] "Abuse of Words," *A Philosophical Dictionary* (London, 1824), I, 37.

[79]

nothing to do with submissiveness to secular tyranny. To prevent misunderstanding, it may be appropriate to state at the start that the political theory of any one thinker is usually decisively influenced by historical circumstances and that theology all too often has been twisted and strained to fit the demands of the hour. The will of God has been identified with the status quo when that status quo was considered agreeable and advantageous for the interests of religion, and God's will has been invoked in support of resistance to the political authority of the day when rulers seriously threatened those same interests. Defenders of absolutism made bad princes the instruments of God's punishment of the people, while spokesmen for popular sovereignty granted that same role to the people, who were similarly seen as executors of the divine will aiming at the downfall of the proud. It is also clear that it is quite impossible to establish a causal relation between theology and politics — between a certain solution to the problem of free will and the affirmation or rejection of resistance. Archbishop Laud and Milton could both be Arminians in their theology while one defended the divine right of kings and the other popular sovereignty.

And yet, the absence of a causal relationship does not mean that these two sets of beliefs are always entirely unrelated. At the very least it seems possible to show that an acceptance of the all-embracing first causality of God can provide strong arguments in support of political quietism, while, on the other hand, a repudiation of the Augustinian determinism makes possible a far more active philosophy of politics, if indeed one desires to avail oneself of the libertarian implications contained in the affirmation of man's moral freedom. A number of illustrations of this twofold thesis are possible.[2]

The link between a deterministic theology and the counsel of submissiveness to tyranny usually consists in the idea of God's regulating evil in the world and using the evil deeds of sinners to punish other sinners. Thus, according to an example given by St. Augustine, the Lord stirred up the Philistines and Arabians against Jehoram and they ravaged the land of Judah.[3] Every evil in the world has to fulfill some good purpose, Augustine insisted; otherwise God, who is all good and of necessity hates sin, would not tolerate it. God appoints the kind of rulers whom he judges people to be worthy of, and, in view of his omnipotence and justice, tyrants must be considered God's retribution for the perversity of the people. Both just kings and cruel tyrants reign by God's providence; none may be resisted.[4]

---

[2] The discussion that follows should not be taken as a full historical account of resistance theories. I have provided examples tending to support the intellectual convergence I seek to elucidate and I have picked and chosen without any attempt at completeness. Moreover, writers proceeding from essentially secular premises like Bartolus and Coluccio Salutati have been omitted as not relevant to the thesis of this study.

[3] "On Grace and Free Will," chap. xlii, *A Select Library of the Nicene and Post-Nicene Fathers of the Christian Church*, ed. Philip Schaff, Vol. V (New York, 1902), p. 462.

[4] *The City of God*, Bk. V, chaps. xix and xxi.

The Augustinian notion of God using sin to punish sin continued to figure prominently in much of medieval thought, including that of St. Thomas Aquinas.

> Every evil that God does, or permits to be done, is directed to some good. But it is not always directed to the good of those in whom the evil is, but sometimes to the good of others, or of the whole universe. Thus He directs the sin of tyrants to the good of the martyrs, and the punishment of the lost to the glory of His justice.[5]

Divine providence has arranged things in such a way that the evil to be found in many human acts will lead to good. God is the author of the evil which is punishment. Justice requires that penalty should be dealt out to sinners.[6] Hence God, as it is said already in Job (34:30), frequently makes a man who is a hypocrite govern because of the sins of the people. "It is as a punishment for sin that, by divine permission, the impious are allowed to rule."[7]

Tyranny, then, is part of God's plan, and private persons may not resist it. "The remedy against the evils of tyranny lies rather in the hands of public authority than in the private judgment of individuals."[8] A king turned tyrant, for example, who has been elected by the community, may be deposed by that community. When human aid against bad rulers is not available, "recourse must be made to God the King of all, and the helper of all who call upon Him in the time of tribulation." But "guilt must first be expiated before the affliction of tyranny can cease," for the ultimate cause of tyranny is the iniquity of the people.[9]

The same view was held in the fourteenth century by Wyclif, whose theology was even more outspokenly Augustinian. It is a grievous sin, the English clergyman insisted, to resist secular authority — be it just or unjust. The rule of tyrants is from God as much as that of good kings. The power

[5] *Summa Theologica,* Ia IIae, qu. 79, art, 4, repl. obj. 1, *Basic Writings,* ed. Anton C. Pegis (New York, 1945), II, 657.

[6] *Ibid.,* I, qu. 49, art. 3.

[7] *De regimine principum,* chap. vi, *Selected Political Writings,* ed. AP. D'Entrèves (Oxford, 1948), p. 35. Cf. on this point Ernst Troeltsch, *The Social Teaching of the Christian Churches,* trans. Olive Wyon (New York, 1949), I, 291.

[8] *De regimine principum,* 31.

[9] *Ibid.,* 33-35. In a passage of the *Commentary on the Sentences of Peter Lombard* (Bk. II, Dist. 44, qu. 2, art. 2, repl. obj. 5), St. Thomas appears to uphold the legitimacy of tyrannicide when no appeal to higher authority is possible. The meaning of this passage has led to numerous literary debates — none of them conclusive. Cf. Jos. Schlecht and B. Duhr, S.J., "Lehre des hl. Thomas über den Tyrannenmord," *Historisches Jahrbuch,* XIV (1893), 107-113. Many of the later scholastics interpreted the passage in question as referring only to the usurper whose force might justly be repelled with force. Cf. Tomasso de Vio, called Cardinal Gaetano, O.P., *Sancti Thomae Aquinatis Secunda Secundae Summae Theologicae . . . cum commentariis Thomas de Vio Caietani,* qu. 64, art, 3 (Rome, 1897).

of the bad is committed to them by God, as is proven by the permission Satan sought to injure Job and the words of Christ to Pilate.[10]

We can find an even more explicit commitment to the doctrines of St. Augustine in the teachings of Luther and Calvin. With Luther, too, man, in his fallen state is thoroughly bad and cannot help doing evil. Human will is guided by God and even man's evil deeds are directed by Him. God does not merely permit sin. The wicked acts of the tyrant are just as much God's doing as the benevolent and just rule of a pious king. Nothing can escape God's all-powerful will. "The will of all men is driven by this action to will or do something, be it good or bad."[11] Why does God not change the bad will? This, Luther answered, belongs to the inscrutability of His decisions. "Here one may not ask. The secrets of God one must honor with adoration."[12]

One possible reason for the prevalence of evil in the world, which Luther suggested, nevertheless, was the use which God made of evil for his own glory and man's benefit. God, for example, ordered Shimei to curse David (II Sam. 16). "In this way God utilized a bad man, in order to deal out a deserved punishment."[13] Now, just as David refused to take vengeance for Shimei's action and forbade his servants to go and kill this member of the house of Saul, we must regard bad rulers as our due and may not oppose them. Man undoubtedly deserves no better, for how else can we understand the prevalence of oppressive tyrants?

> The world is far too wicked to be worthy of good and pious lords, it must have princes who go to war, levy taxes and shed blood, and it must have spiritual tyrants who impoverish and burden it with bulls and letters and laws. This and other chastisements are rather what it has deserved, and to resist them is nothing else than to resist God's chastisement. As humbly as I conduct myself when God sends me a sickness, so humbly should I conduct myself toward the evil government which the same God also sends me.[14]

---

[10] Iohannis Wyclif, *Tractatus de officio regis,* chap. i (London, 1887), p. 8: "Unde quod perversorum potestas non sit nisi a deo patet Job ii, ubi diabolus antequam aliquid beato Job tolleret dicebat domino *Mitte manum tuam,* id est da potestatem. Et istam sentenciam inculcat veritas pilato dicens Johannis xix sic: *No haberes potestatem adversus me ullam nisi datum esset tibi desuper."*

[11] Martin Luther, *Vom unfreien Willen,* ed. Otto Schumacher (Göttingen, 1937), p. 182. For a good discussion of Luther's doctrine of the bondage of the will see Christoph Ernst Luthardt, *Die Lehre vom freien Willen und seinem Verhältnis zur Gnade in ihrer geschichtlichen Entwicklung dargestellt* (Leipzig, 1863).

[12] Luther, *Vom unfreien Willen,* p. 140.

[13] *Ibid.,* 138.

[14] "A Treatise concerning the Ban," *Works of Martin Luther,* Vol. II (Philadelphia, 1943), p. 51. Luther was answered more than two hundred years later by Rousseau in *The Social Contract:* "All power comes from God, I admit; but so does all sickness: does that mean that we are forbidden to call in the doctor?" (Bk. I, chap. iii, trans. G. D. H. Cole). See on this point also Jacques-François Thomas, *Le pelagianisme de J. J. Rousseau* (Paris, 1956).

To be sure, Luther granted the right to disobey commands manifestly against the word of God. He also admonished princes to be good and pious, and, in the latter part of his life, recognized the right of the Electors to depose the Emperor. But all this remained irrelevant to the duty of the subject not to resist temporal authority. All princes were God's tools and part of the divine plan. "They are God's jailers and hangmen," he said on another occasion, "and His divine wrath needs them to punish the wicked and preserve outward peace."[15] A deterministic theology, which denied man's free will and saw in every action of man God's omnipotent guidance, ended in a political ethic of submission.[16] Luther admonished man to accept tyrants as humbly as disease. To be consistent, Luther should have advised the sick man against the taking of medicine.

In the case of Calvin, a very similar theology was accompanied by like counsel in the sphere of politics. In Calvin's religion, too, man has no free will and all things come to pass through the efficacious providence of God. Man's fate is predestined and nothing can change God's inscrutable judgment. Again, Calvin was as emphatic as Luther about the sin involved in resisting tyranny. Even the most iniquitous tyrants derive their power from God, and it is positively seditious for individuals to treat kings according to their merits.[17] When harassed by cruel princes, we must call to mind our transgressions against God, for which we are punished by these scourges, and implore God's aid. In addition to the "magistrates appointed for the protection of the people" to "check the undue license of kings . . . when they tyrannise over the humbler of the people"[13] there remains merely prayer to God who sometimes "raises up manifest avengers from among his own servants" or "employs, for this purpose, the fury of men who have other

---

[15] "Secular Authority: To what extent it should be obeyed," *Works*, III, 258.

[16] In all justice, it should be noted here that the early Protestant emphasis on the doctrine of absolute predestination also had another effect — it deprecated the institutional aspect of the Church and thus, at least indirectly, included a tendency of encouraging individualism. The idea of predestination, Troeltsch observes, had "a disintegrating effect upon the idea of the Church as the ecclesiastical organ of salvation," it "exalted the individual and personal immediacy of the soul's relationship with God — a relationship which is the work of God, and not of the Church, and about whose existence God, and not the Church, decides" (Troeltsch, I, 360). The English Antinomians during the Puritan Revolution similarly contributed to political liberty by being champions of the individual conscience. "By opposing the interference of the civil magistrates in religious affairs," writes Leo F. Solt, "the chaplains introduced an element of human responsibility into an otherwise deterministic theological scheme" (*Saints in Arms: Puritanism and Democracy in Cromwell's Army* [Stanford, Cal., 1959], p. 47). Much of the original Protestant stress on non-resistance can also probably be traced to the reformers' literal interpretation of Scripture into which they were forced by their revolt against the Church and in favor of Holy Writ — hence, for example, the strict adherence to Romans xiii. Only with the passage of time and the maturing of Bibliolatry did Protestantism, like Catholicism earlier, find ways to interpret away some difficulties stemming from Biblical literalism and attain some much needed political flexibility.

[17] John Calvin, *Institutes of the Christian Religion*, Bk. IV, chap. xx, sec. 27, trans. Henry Beveridge (Grand Rapids, Mich., 1953), II, 672.

[18] *Ibid.*, 31, II, 675.

thoughts and other aims."[19]   In this way God tamed the insolence of the Egyptians by the might of the Assyrians, who did His work without knowing it.

The God of the Protestants, a recent student of sixteenth century political thought correctly notes, "was always taking direct action in the world. If a tyrant existed it was because God had work for him to do; and if God did not want the tyrant, God could be relied upon to remove him, as He had removed Sennacherib and Ahab, Nebuchadnezar and Herod."[20]   The will of God was the supreme and, for practical purposes, sole causality of all human affairs.

Not surprisingly, many of the French Calvinists granted to the magistrates and not to "particular and private persons" the right of resisting legitimate rulers who had fallen into tyranny. If the magistrates fail in their duty, the *Vindiciae Contra Tyrannos* insisted, "let private men remember the saying of Job, 'That for the sins of the people God permits hypocrites to reign,' whom it is impossible either to convert or subvert, if man repent not of their ways, to walk in obedience to God's commandments."[21]   In such a case, the people have only the weapon of bended knees and humble prayer, "persuading themselves that an outrageous tyranny is to be supported as patiently, as some exceeding damage done by the violence of tempests, or excessive overflowing waters."[22]   The affirmation of rebellion by John Knox was couched in even more cautious terminology. His appeal was primarily to the Scottish nobility and the right of resistance to tyranny for secular causes was explicitly rejected.[23]   Knox's ire was really directed against idolatry and the call for resistance to blasphemous princes was but an aspect of the duty of punishing all those — whatever their station — who subvert the true religion.

If the denial of human free will and stress on the efficacious providence of God were especially well suited for the rejection of the rightfulness of individual resistance to tyranny, the affirmation of man's moral freedom supplied a powerful support for the espousal of just this right. With the responsibility for sin placed squarely on the shoulders of the sinner, it is easier to defend resistance to the sinful and unjust actions of bad rulers and to repudiate the argument that tyranny constitutes God's retribution which

---

[19] *Ibid.,* 30, II, 674. Cf. St. Augstine, *The City of God,* I, xxi.

[20] Christopher Morris, *Political Thought in England: Tyndale to Hooker* (London, 1953), p. 42.

[21] Junius Brutus, *A Defence of Liberty Against Tyrants,* ed. Harold J. Laski (London, 1924), p. 210.

[22] *Ibid.* It is interesting to note that Du Plessis Mornay, to whom the authorship of the *Vindiciae* is frequently attributed, apparently was not a very strict Calvinist and did his best to try to heal the breach between the Arminians and the orthodox Dutch Calvinist party. Cf. A. W. Harrison, *The Beginnings of Arminianism: To the Synod of Dort* (London, 1926), pp. 233 and 256.

[23] "A Letter Addressed to the Commonalty of Scotland," *The Works of John Knox,* ed. David Laing (Edinburgh, 1864), IV, 532. Cf. J. H. Burns, "The Political Ideas of the Scottish Reformation," *Aberdeen University Review,* XXXVI (1956), 263.

may not be opposed. This, for example, was the line of thought of the Jesuit Suárez when taking issue with Luther's political quietism. "The statement of Luther that it is not lawful to resist the punishment of God is indeed ridiculous for God does not will the evils but merely permits them; and therefore He does not forbid that they should be justly repelled."[24] God cannot be expectetd to punish a tyrant any more than a thief.

The Spanish Jesuit Juan de Mariana, one of the greatest systematic exponents of the right of resistance to tyranny in the sixteenth century,[25] developed an even more radical theological position on predestination and the origin of evil. Mariana made no secret of his admiration for the Semi-Pelagians Cassian and Faustus whom he called "outstanding men."[26] Their teaching on predestination, grace and free will, he noted, was the same as that of other fathers of the Church. Conditional, rather than absolute, predestination befits the goodness of a God, who wants all men to be saved. Indeed, even from among those not originally belonging to the predestined some will be saved, if they themselves want it.[27] Man can do some good on his own and thus, as it were, help along his salvation. We should beware, Mariana cautioned, "of attributing everything to God's help, so that we will be left with nothing but depravity and an evil human nature."[28]

[24] Francisco Suárez, De bello, sec. I, no. 5, Selections from Three Works, ed. James Brown Scott (Oxford, 1944), II, 804.

Suárez's argument resembles the view of the famous medieval theologian Peter Abélard according to whom princes receive their power to rule justly from God but act cruelly out of their own evil nature:

> It is one thing to resist the tyranny of an evil ruler, another to resist his just power which he has received from God. For when he plunges into violence as does not pertain to his power and the terms of his office, and we resist him in this, we oppose his tyranny rather than his power, man rather than God, since he presumes thus to act on his own and not according to the will of God.

Commentarii super S. Pauli epistolam ad Romanos libri V, lib. IV, Opera, ed. Victor Cousin (Paris, 1859), II, 322. Abélard himself has frequently been accused of leaning toward Pelagianism because of his assertion that man by his unaided free will is able to do some good. See ibid., II, 292 and Capitula errorum Petri Abaelardi, no. VI, Opera, II, 767.

[25] For Mariana's views on the right of resistance and tyrannicide see his De rege et regis institutione (Toledo, 1599), especially lib. I, caps. vi and vii, and Guenter Lewy, Constitutionalism and Statecraft During the Golden Age of Spain: A Study of the Political Philosophy of Juan de Mariana, S.J. (Geneva, 1960), ch. 5.

[26] Juan de Mariana, S.J., De morte et immortalitate, lib. III, cap. vi, Tractatus VII (Cologne, 1609), p. 430.

After Pelagianism had been condemned by the Church as heretical in 431 A.D., its place in the struggle against Augustinianism was taken over by another faction. The so-called Semi-Pelagian school arose, led first by the French abbot John Cassian and a little later by Bishop Faustus of Rhegium (Riez). Stressing that God wills the salvation of all, these theologians insisted that man's free will is never destroyed by God. While conceding the importance of divine grace, they asserted that God frequently awaits the unaided impulses of human beings before coming to their assistance. There thus exists a certain claim to grace based on purely human effort. See Gustav Friedrich Wiggers, Versuch einer pragmatischen Darstellung des Semipelagianismus in seinem Kampfe gegen den Augustinismus bis zur zweiten Synode zu Orange (Hamburg, 1833).

[27] De morte, viii, 437.

[28] Ibid., xi, 438.

Mariana's position on the question of the origin of evil, on the other hand, essentially followed the new doctrine of Molinism, so called after its first great systematic exponent, Luis Molina.[29] God is not the author of evil, but merely permits it. He allows evil to exist, without, however, sanctioning it or predetermining the precise circumstances of any particular sin. Man is free to do good or evil and the responsibility for sin is exclusively ours. Evildoers, warns Mariana, "should not take refuge in divine permission and seek in it a place to hide."[30] The implications of this sentence for Mariana's affirmation of tyrannicide are suggestive.

"The doctrine of predestination in its original Calvinistic meaning," writes Sabine, "tied up all moral and social questions with the free grace of God and made every natural phenomenon an incident in a personal and voluntary government of the world."[31] Small wonder that many later Protestants, once the pressure of persecution dictated the abandonment of the doctrine of non-resistance, undertook to modify the doctrine of the total depravity of man. "The development of the whole controversy [over the legitimacy of resistance]," J. W. Allen observes, "is one of the most striking examples of the way in which men adjust their theories at once to their desires and to circumstances."[32]

One of the first to break with the doctrine of the bondage of the will was Thomas Müntzer, who participated prominently in the German peasant revolt of 1525. Müntzer preached the complete fulfillment of God's law on earth, the rule of the elect, and the punishment of the godless, including temporal rulers. The latter must not be allowed to plead God's ordination. Müntzer objected to Luther's interpretation of Scripture, which "makes God

---

[29] The Jesuit Molina in his book *Concordia liberi arbitrii cum gratiae donis, divina praescientia providentia praedestinatione et reprobatione,* published in 1588, attempted to reconcile God's prescience with man's free will by way of a divine knowledge of future conditionals which he called *scientia media.* Molina also insisted that those predestined are so not because of the efficacy of a divine decree, but because of the consent of human will to the saving grace of God. In turn, those not chosen were seen lost because of the sinner's own actions.

Molinism soon became the quasi-official position of the Jesuits, who wished to be radically different not only from their chief enemy, Protestantism, but also from their great rivals in the Church, the Dominicans. "It was mortifying to the Jesuits," writes Ranke, "to follow in the train of the Dominicans, to whom St. Thomas had belonged, and who were regarded as the natural expositors of his opinions" (*History of the Popes,* II, 87). Also the Augustinian formulation of the problem of free will was ill adapted to the needs of a propagandistic order. Their aims were the restoration of Catholicism in Europe and its propagation in the pagan world beyond. To achieve this goal they had to hold out hope for the ultimate salvation of *all* men and not only of the predestined. (Cf. Loyola's fifteenth rule for thinking with the Church in the *Spiritual Exercises* where he warns the Order against talking too much about predestination.) Moreover, one of their greatest weapons soon became the confessional, and full utilization of this tool again dictated the assertion of free will and the efficacy of human effort.

[30] *De morte,* II, xii, 414.

[31] George H. Sabine, *A History of Political Theory,* (rev. ed.; New York 1950), p. 416.

[32] *A History of Political Thought in the Sixteenth Century* (London, 1951), p. 304.

the author of evil" and "shamefully despises man's free will."[33] God in his goodness, Müntzer taught, wills the salvation of all believers and does not know a decree to reprobation.[34] The same theological views were upheld by the Anabaptists. The radical faction of Anabaptism in particular, desirous of building the kingdom of God on earth, if necessary by force, could not afford to tolerate doubts about the ability of man's will to realize the good to achieve salvation by personal effort. The destruction of the ungodly, the revolutionary Anabaptists felt, would accomplish the will of God and contribute to their own deliverance. The time of vengeance had come, declared Bernhardt Rothmann, one of the leaders of the New Jerusalem at Münster, in 1534. He called on his followers to arm themselves "not only with the apostle's weapon of patience in suffering, but also with the glorious armor of David, to vengeance, so that you may, with God's might and help, root out the power of Babylon and all the godless world."[35]

A doctrine of the divine right of rebellion was developed in the German city of Magdeburg when it was threatened by the forces of the Emperor in 1547. In this so-called *Bekenntnis* of Magdeburg, composed by a number of Lutheran ministers, the affirmation of the rightfulness of resisting tyranny brought with it a definite rejection of Luther's views on tyranny and the origin of sin. God, it was argued, has granted authority to command for the sake of justice and truth; He has not given authority to abolish true religion or unjustly to take from subjects their lives and property. In such cases, resistance by force is justified. To deny this right is to assume that God wills the maintenance of evil and commands disobedience to Himself.[36]

The Calvinist camp was somewhat slower in undertaking the readjustment of theological precepts inimical to active resistance. Much of the incoherence in the writings of the Huguenots following the massacre of St. Bartholomew in 1572, Allen remarks, stems from the difficult task of reconciling Calvinistic modes of thought with traditional medieval teaching on the right of rebellion.[37] Beza, for example, held on to the view that tyranny is an evil sent by God to punish His people, for which the proper remedy is prayer and repentance; yet he added that this did not rule out the use of other just measures.[38] Nothing can exist without divine approval, Beza conceded, but why could it not be God's will that tyrants be punished by the

---

[33] Thomas Müntzer, "Hochverursachte Schutzrede," *Politische Schriften,* ed. Carl Hinrichs (Halle, 1950), p. 95.

[34] *Ibid.,* p. 82.

[35] Bernhardt Rothmann, *Büchlein von der Rache,* cited in Ulrich Bergfried, *Verantwortung als theologisches Problem im Täufertum des 16, Jahrhunderts* (Wuppertal, 1938), p. 148.

[36] Nicolaus von Amsdorf *et al., Confessio et apologia pastorum et reliquorum ministrorum ecclesiae Magdeburgensis,* Part II, argument 3 (Magdeburg, 1550), pp. G3-G4.

[37] Allen, p. 313.

[38] Theodore de Bèze, *Du droit des magistrats sur leurs sujets* in Simon Goulart, ed., *Memoires de l'estat de France sous Charles IX* (Meidelbourg, 1578), II, 488.

people rather than the people by tyrants?[39] In an attempt to remain faithful to his master's teaching on the subject of tyranny and yet, at the same time, to justify the resistance of the French Calvinists, Beza fell back upon an argument that indeed could be used to rationalize any and all courses of human conduct.

John Ponet, Bishop of Winchester under Edward VI and later another of the Marian exiles, definitely broke with orthodox Calvinism. His defense of resistance to tyranny consequently could be far more forceful and was not limited to the magistrates. Ponet explicitly rejected the argument that God sends tyrants as punishment for the people's wickedness. To assume that would make "God the author of evil: which were a great blasphemie."[40] Tyrants have no divine mandate and may rightfully be killed. By the time of the Puritan Revolution even a staunch Presbyterian like Samuel Rutherford might deny the view that both good and evil in the world are to be considered as God's doing. The political conclusion, which Rutherford wanted to reach, now followed logically: "Tyranny being a work of Satan, is not from God because sin, either habitual or actual, is not from God."[41] An absolute power to tyrannize cannot be considered as being in conformity with God's will because "if this moral power to sin be from God, it being formally wickedness, God must be the author of sin."[42]

The Independent Milton had largely emancipated himself from Calvin's theology and took an even more forthright stand in the politics of the revolution.[43] The famous poet, a Christian humanist, fervently believed in the natural dignity of man and in the power and freedom of the human will. His *De Doctrina Christiana* was written from an outright Arminian standpoint. Reprobation, Milton declared, "forms no part of what is meant by the divine predestination."[44] All those who believe will be saved; none will be lost except through his own fault. Predestination is general and conditional, not particular and absolute. If we were to assume that God "inclines the will of man to moral good or evil, according to his own pleasure, and then rewards the good, and punishes the wicked, the course of equity seems

---

[39] *Ibid.,* 516. Beza here resurrects an old idea. Already around 1100 Hugh of Fleury had taught in his *De regia potestate* that God punishes bad princes by the insubordination of their peoples. Cf. Friedrich August Freiherr von der Heydte, *Die Geburtsstunde des souveränen Staates* (Regensburg, 1952), p. 365, n. 89.
[40] John Ponet, *A Short Treatise of Politike Power*, Facsimile reproduction in Winthrop S. Hudson, *John Ponet (1516?-1556): Advocate of Limited Monarchy* (Chicago, 1942), p. 43.
[41] Samuel Rutherford, *Lex, Rex, or The Law and The Prince,* Question IX (Edinburgh, 1843), p. 34.
[42] *Ibid.,* XXII, 102.
[43] For a good discussion of Milton's political ideas see Don M. Wolfe, *Milton in the Puritan Revolution* (New York, 1941) and Arthur E. Barker, *Milton and the Puritan Dilemma* (Toronto, 1942). Milton's theory of evil is treated by Peter F. Fisher, "Milton's Theodicy," *Journal of the History of Ideas,* XVII (1956), 28-53.
[44] *De Doctrina Christiana,* Bk. I, chap. iv, *The Works of John Milton,* ed. Frank Allen Patterson (New York, 1933), XIV, 101.

to be disturbed."[45] Man alone is responsible for all his actions. God merely foreknows all future events, he does not decree them necessarily, "lest the consequence should be that sin in general would be imputed to the Deity, and evil spirits and wicked men exempt from blame."[46]

The same spirit of rebellious individualism and passionate belief in freedom is found in Milton's political ideas. Man's destiny, Milton argued, is in his own hands not only as pertains to salvation, but also in earthly affairs. He defended the right of the people of England to execute their tyrannical king. Like Ponet, Milton rejected the argument that God appoints rulers suitable to the qualities of the people. The people themselves have the right to choose and change their governors. Moreover, "we read that frequently a bad king was given to a good people, and contrariwise, a good king to a bad people."[47]

Milton took sharp issue with the suggestion that God had put the English nation in slavery to Charles Stuart and that only God therefore could be relied upon to release it.

> That God allowed them I would not deny, but I have never heard that he gave them. Or if God be said to give a people into slavery whenever a tyrant prevails over the people, why ought he not as well be said to set them free whenever the people prevail over a tyrant? Shall the tyrant credit and owe his tyranny to God, and not we our liberty? There is no evil in the state that the Lord hath not let in, Amos 3. Famine, plague, sedition, a public enemy — is there a single one of these that the state will not strive with all its might to shake off? Shake them off it surely will if it can, though it know them to be sent by God, unless himself from heaven should command the contrary. Upon the same reasoning why may not the state rid itself of a tyrant if it be stronger than he? Why should we suppose the uncontrolled passions of the one man to be appointed by God for the common ill, rather than the self-controlled power of the whole state for the common weal?[48]

God sets up one kingdom and pulls down another, Milton conceded, but men are his instruments. Man cannot rely on prayer alone to ward off misery and injustice. "For who that is hardpressed by misfortune merely cried out to God, and does naught but fall to his lazy prayers so as to neglect all else his duty?"[49] As to the argument of Knox that rebellion is allowed only in matters of spiritual concern, Milton asked why unlimited power in one man should be considered less destructive in temporal than in religious affairs. "Does God really concern himself nowise with civil affairs? If he does not,

---

[45] *Ibid.*, chap. xii, pp. 213-215.
[46] *Ibid.*, iii, 85.
[47] *Defence of the People of England,* chap. iii, *Works,* VII, 191.
[48] *Ibid.*, pp. 179-181.
[49] *Ibid.*, chap. ii, p. 101.

surely he does not forbid us to take care of them. If he does, he would have the same reformation made in the commonwealth as in the church."[50]

Augustinian theology divided the world into saved and reprobate. Both salvation and reprobation depended upon an absolute and irresistible divine decree. In the eyes of the Semi-Pelagians, Molinists, and Arminians, this doctrine was inequitable and made God the author of sin. Justice could not tolerate the condemnation of man for sins which were committed without his personal responsibility. Arminianism, in particular, stressed the need to submit God's actions to more rational analysis. It expressed a psychology of rationalistic optimism that trusted the capacity of human effort and free will to do good and achieve salvation. A theology such as this, which unequivocally excluded evil and sin from the divine determinism, was of great help to those defenders of the right of resistance to tyranny whose political thought was but an integral part of their theological speculation.

Again, this is not to say that all Christian theologians defending free will were political radicals, or that all those thinkers who affirmed the right of resistance held heretical views on the question of grace and predestination. It would be a great mistake to ignore purely political factors like Augustine's desire to obtain secular support for the suppression of heresy and Luther's need of assistance from the princes of the Empire in trying to account for the conservative character of their political thought. It would seem, nevertheless, that theology frequently provides a framework for political philosophy. Certain positions on the question of man's relation to God become relevant to specific formulations of the problem of man's relation to man in the human community. The views of St. Augustine, Luther, Suárez, Mariana, and Milton are obvious cases in point. In this sense, theology and politics are complementary and often depend one upon the other.

[50] *Ibid.*, iii, 209-211.

LITERARY AND POLITICAL SATIRE IN TIRSO'S
"LA FINGIDA ARCADIA"

Ruth L. Kennedy

Professor Emeritus of Spanish Literature,

Smith College

Tirso's *La fingida Arcadia*[1] is, on the surface, a pastoral play which exalts Lope de Vega while satirizing most of the groups inimical to him. The blows therein are directed primarily against the *tramoyistas,* though the Gongorists, and even the Aristotelians, come in for their share of pummelling.[2] What has not been suspected, in so far as I know, is that the satire of the *tramoyistas* in this *comedia* is directed specifically against Luis Vélez de Guevara — and, through him, at the Count-Duke of Olivares: in other words, Tirso's scenes have political, as well as literary, significance. In establishing this connection, we shall not only point the way to further understanding of Tirso's attitude toward Philip IV's favorite — an attitude which in 1625 was to result in the Mercedarian's banishment from Madrid — but shall get a glimpse into his relations with the palace clique of Andalusian poets who looked to that magnate as their Maecenas at court.

That there were bad relations between Tirso and Vélez de Guevara has scarcely been noted, and the bases on which I assert its existence will at first seem very slight indeed. In January of 1626, as the King was setting out for Zaragoza, Vélez, *pedigüeño* as always,[3] begs his sovereign for a new suit in order that he may accompany him. In return for the favor, he promises to be:[4]

> en todo el Pentecostés,
> de las alabanzas vuestras,
> eterno versifiquier,
> más digna haciendo su musa
> del siempre verde laurel.

---

[1] Princeps: *Parte III* (Tortosa, 1634). All references in this study are to the edition of E. Cortarelo y Mori, *NBAE,* IV (Madrid, 1906), 434-459. All other allusions to Tirso's plays found in this study are to *BAE,* V and *NBAE,* IV and IX, unless it is stated otherwise.

[2] For satire against the *tramoyistas,* see III, iii, 454-455, and xii, 459; for that of the Gongorists, III iii, 454; and for that of the Aristotelians, I, i, 434.

[3] Vélez's habits in this direction were so well known that Lope, on asking the Duque de Sesa for a *sotana,* comments: "Parece cosa de Luis Vélez." Amezúa, *Epistolario de Lope de Vega Carpio,* IV (Madrid, 1943), 17.

[4] Quoted by Rodríguez-Marín, *RABM,* XIX (1908), 62-78; specifically p. 75 with the title, "Cinco poesías autobiográficas de Luis Vélez de Guevara." I quoted these verses in *"La prudencia en la mujer* and the Ambient that Brought it Forth," *PMLA,* LXIII (1948), 1187.

And he ends this promise with the following curse:

> Malos años para Arceo
> y *el fraile de la Merced!*

With the enmity that existed between Vélez and *Arceo,* we are not here concerned; with that he felt for *el fraile de la Merced* (i.e., Tirso)[5] we are.

In Tirso's theatre there are likewise two lines which have on occasion been interpreted as a possible slap aimed in the direction of Luis Vélez de Guevara. *La celosa de sí misma,* written in late 1622 or early 1623[6], includes the following satirical verses of the *gracioso* Ventura, made when the veiled doña Magdalena approaches his master, don Melchor (*BAE,* V, Act II, iv, 137):

> Sé sumiller de cortina:
> descubre aquesa *apariencia,*[7]
> tocarán las chirimías;
> *que en las tramoyas pareces*
> *poeta de Andalucía.*

Don Emilio Cotarelo, pointing to the last two lines of this quotation, declares[8] in connection with Vélez's love of the spectacular: ". . . parece ser influjo de la tierra. Por eso, decía el personaje de la comedia de Tirso: 'en las tramoyas pareces / poeta de Andalucía.' " I believe him eminently right in this assumption.

With these two slight leads to point the way — plus the realization that Tirso was by 1622 bitterly critical of Olivares and his regime[9] — let us see if we can unravel some fascinating satire in *La fingida Arcadia,* as well as the literary and political tensions that lay behind it. This play, which has as its general background the war in the Valtelline — as do various other Tirsescan *comedias* of this same general epoch — was clearly done as a *particular,*

---

[5] The term was the usual one applied to Tirso: see, for instance, *BAE,* V, 520c. Moreover, when the *Junta de Reformación* banished Tirso, it used the term "fraile mercedario." See *BRAE,* XXV (1946), 83. It was possibly this anonymity to which Tirso was objecting when in writing *Antona García* he complained, through the Seventh Castilian, that envy had robbed him even of a name ("que hasta el nombre me quito / la envidia.") See III, ii, 635.

[6] See *HR,* X (1942), 209-214.

[7] This term *aparienca* must originally have referred to a stationary setting which could be revealed to the audience by running or raising a curtain. The *aparienca* probably first appeared in connection with *vidas de santos* wherein there was an apparition of the Virgin or of some saint, at which moment *chirimías* were heard. Apparently, when Rojas was writing his *Viaje entretenido,* it was not an identical term with *tramoya,* which implied stage machinery. Speaking of the *vidas de santos* and the *farsas de guerra,* Rojas wrote: "Llegó el tiempo que se usaron / las comedias de *apariencias* / de santos y de *tramoyas* / y entre éstas, farsas de guerra." Quoted from Rennert, *The Spanish Stage* (N.Y., 1909), 79, n. 1. Later, *apariencia, tramoya,* and *invención* seem to be used interchangeably.

[8] See E. Cortarelo, "Luis Vélez de Guevara y sus obras dramáticas," in *Bol. Ac. Esp.,* III (1917), 621-652 and IV (1918), 137-171, 269-308, 414-444. For quotation given, see III, 637.

[9] For this enmity, see my study on *La prudencia en la mujer* (cited above), 1173-1175; also "Notes on Two Interrelated Plays: *El amor y el amistad* and *Ventura te dé Dios, hijo,*" *HR,* XXVIII (1960), 212-13.

one that was played in the confines of a private garden or patio.[10]   It was written, first to celebrate the marriage of don Felipe Centellas to an Italian countess, named Lucrecia;[11] and, secondly, to welcome the arrival of don Jerónimo Pimentel,[12] Captain-general of the Cavalry in northern Italy, who held that position under the command of the great Duque de Feria.[13]

On writing *La fingida Arcadia,* wherein he exalts Lope in such glowing terms that it almost seems a burlesque at times, Tirso has taken his framework from the latter's novel, *La Arcadia* — a debt that he acknowledges repeatedly within the lines of the play itself.[14]   The heroine of Tirso's *comedia* is a romantic young miss — one who like thousands of other young girls of the time, found their *ars amoris* in Lope's poetry.   In the opening scene it is evident that her bed-side table had, through the years, been laden not with the various religious manuals recommended by Fathers of the Church (which would make clear to her her role as future wife and mother) but instead with Lope's *comedias.*   She is his warm admirer, his fervent defender, and in the first scene she names his works almost one by one.   What is more, she knows the basic issue involved in his fight with Torres Rámila, the classicist: having arrived at *La Filomela* of 1621[15] — wherein Lope satirized that unwise grammarian, she even picks up, disdainfully, the phrase "infusa ciencia," which Lope had put into Torres' mouth (I, i, 484a.):

> a él [i.e., a Lope] le da más alabanza
> lo que por su ingenio alcanza
> que a esotro su *ciencia infusa.*

[10] See Felipe's comment (I, v, 440): "No trocaré desde hoy más / estos jardines elisios / . . . por la silla del imperio." The second act upens with scenes that evidently take place in the garden: Felipe is *amante jardinero* and is planting *maravillas, espuelas de caballero,* etc.   Much of act III must also have been played in the open: scene iii has in its stage directions: "y queda un jardín lleno de flores y yedra."   See below, n. 54.
That this play was not put on in the public theatres is suggested also by the fact that in the various lists of comedias we have of the twenties — those of the Palace in 1622-23, Roque de Figueroa's, Juan Acacio's, Amella's, etc. — there is no *Fingida Arcadia* listed.
[11] My attempts in Italy some years ago to identify Lucrecia were unsuccessful, possibly because at that time I made search in 1621, not 1622. The Centellas were of the Oliva family, which was linked up by marriage with the Borjas. For a note on the Centellas, see my study on *La prudencia,* p. 1184.
[12] I have previously had occasion to deal with *La fingida Arcadia* and the Pimentels. See "On the date of Five Plays by Tirso," *HR,* X (1942), 191-199 and the one on *La prudencia* (quoted above), 1181-1186.
[13] The Duque in question was the third of that house.   He had as family name Lorenzo Suárez de Figueroa, the same as that of his father, the second Duque de Feria, who had been ambassador in Rome and France, Viceroy and Captain-general of Cataluña and Sicily. The Duque de Feria, of whom Tirso speaks, was governor of Milán and Viceroy of Valencia and Sicily. He died in 1634 (*Enciclopedia Espasa,* under "Feria").
[14] See in particular I, i, ii and III, iii, xii.
[15] The *aprobación* is Vicente Espinel's, dated May 31, 1621, and the *tasa,* July 19, 1621. It is dedicated to Leonor Pimental.
For a study of Lope's relations with the Aristotelians, see Joaquín de Entrambasaguas, "Una guerra literaria del Siglo de Oro," included in his *Estudios sobre Lope de Vega,* I and II.

Esotro is Torres Rámila, *el tordo,* and his *ciencia infusa* is a clear reflection of the battle between the Aristotelians, who are exalting literary training (*el arte*), and the *lopistas,* who chose to throw the emphasis on inborn talent (*el natural*).[16]

In the third act of his play (iii, 454) Tirso takes up the other two groups who were challenging Lope's supremacy. He first disposes of Góngora and the *gongorinos.* Amplifying the *Parnaso crítico,* which he had previously used in his *Cigarrales,*[17] Tirso here fashions a *Parnaso de Apolo,* made up of three parts: Purgatory, Hell, and Glory. He has assigned to Purgatory the followers of the Cordoban, "los más de ellos . . . ignorantes." But Góngora himself, as the dogmatist who has introduced a new heretical sect, is in Hell, and with him the new Latinized words and metaphors he has coined, such as: *candor, brillante, émulo, coturno, celaje, cristal, animado, hipérbole, pululante, palestra, giro, cerúleo, crepúsculos, y fragrantes.* With Tirso's satire of this group, we are not here concerned; our interest on this occasion must, like Tirso's, be centered upon a third literary group, i.e., the *tramoyistas,* who are likewise in Hell along with Góngora.

Before dealing with Tirso's satire against this group, we must first study its immediate sources. Again, we shall find them in Lope. The last *Parte* of *comedias* which Lucrecia mentions, in checking off Lope's works, is his *Décima séptima,* one whose *fe de erratas* is dated January 25, 1621. It came out some ten months before the *Parte XVI,* which could not have reached the public before the last two weeks of December, 1621.[18] Tirso makes no mention whatsoever of this *Parte,* but he undoubtedly had read its prologue, as well as one play therein, before writing *La fingida Arcadia.* In the preliminary pages to this volume, Lope has included a "prólogo dialogístico [sic]," which takes place between *Teatro* and *Forastero.* Therein *Teatro* complains that he is maimed:[19] "my legs and arms are broken," he says; "I am full of holes and with a thousand trap doors and nails, a miserable plight which is due to the carpenters by order of the theatrical managers." *Forastero* then protests that it is not the theatrical managers who should be blamed; rather, such conditions are due, as he sees it, to the dramatists who are like the physicians and barbers of the day: they give orders, and the patient bleeds. *Teatro* half agrees, but after all, what can the poets and managers do "if all the great actors, such as Cisneros, Sandoval, and Cristobal, are now dead, and

[16] I have a long study in manuscript on Tirso's relations with this same group. If the Mercedarian says little here of the *Aristotélicos,* it is because he had already expressed his disdain for them, or was on the point of doing so, in the *Cigarrales,* the *Bandolero,* and *Ventura te dé Dios, hijo.*

[17] Ed. Espasa-Calpe (Madrid, 1942), I, 113-117.

[18] Vicente Espinel approved it on September 24, 1620. Its *suma del privilegio* is dated October 24, 1620; its *tasa,* September 27, 1621, and its *erratas,* December 15, 1621.

[19] This dialogue is quoted, in part, from Rennert's *The Life of Lope de Vega* (Glasgow, 1904), 288-291. I have occasionally altered the wording of the translation and have eliminated such parts as are not germane to my purpose.

if audiences come to *see* rather than to *hear?* If the public wants *spectacle* rather than *poetry,* the managers must necessarily take refuge in *tramoyas* and *volatines,* and the poets in conceits that are strained ('a los aros de cedazo')." *Teatro* adds that he could understand the public's delight in stage machinery, were it managed cleverly as in the days of Euripides, Aeschylus, and Sophocles; but how *can* it be charmed by such crude stuff as is being used for the Spanish *comedia* where the *figuras* rise and descend so awkwardly and where animals and birds appear in similar fashion?

But there is more, for this *Sixteenth Part* contains a play called *Lo fingido verdadero.* It is the life of San Ginés, an *autor de comedias* in Diocletian's time, who was put in the calendar of the church's saints after being burned as a Christian. Significantly, this play carries a dedication to Tirso de Molina.[20] The protagonist of this *vida de santo,* first written around 1608-1609,[21] when Lope was defending himself in the *Arte nuevo de hacer comedias* against the attacks of the classicists, has been summoned to court to put on a play before the Emperor (II, 57-58). Ginés, as *impresario,* first offers to put on one of Terence or Plautus, but Diocletian rejects the suggestion, even if such plays do follow established precepts for the *comedia* and thus conform to Aristotelian canons. Ginés then suggests *La contienda de Marsias y de Apolo,*[22] whose author is Corintio, "hombre fantástico," he says, "en la pintura de furiosos versos . . . digno de oír en lo que acierta pero infeliz en las trazas e invenciones." When this suggestion also proves unacceptable to the Emperor, he proposes one of a Greek poet, "*que las funda todas en subir y bajar monstruos al cielo.*"[23] He adds (II, 58): "El teatro parece un escritorio / con diversas navetas y cortinas; / no hay tabla de ajedrez como su lienzo." And he closes his strictures with the following comment: ". . . suelen espantar al vulgo rudo / y darnos más dinero que las buenas, / porque habla en necio, y aunque dos se ofendan / quedan más de quinientos que la atiendan." Significantly, Diocletian ends up by asking for one of love, that is, one that conformed to the Lopean formula for the *capa y espada.* And this, as we shall see, is what both Lope and Tirso were still urging in the 20's — against the play of *tramoyas* favored by the Andalusians.

Master of ceremonies for the *Parnaso de Apolo,* which Tirso has included in the third act of *La fingida Arcadia,* is the *gracioso* Pinzón, who is

[20] It may be read in Pérez Pastor, *Bibl. Madr.,* III, 66.

[21] See Morley and Bruerton, *The Chronology of Lope de Vega's "comedias"* (N.Y., 1940), 198. They date it "ca.1608."

[22] La "contienda de Marsias y de Apolo" was a theme that Lope was to mention in his struggle with Torres Rámila (See Entrambasaguas, *op. cit.,* II, 43). I feel it not improbable that Lope may have altered somewhat this passage at the time he sent it to print in 1620. Corintio is possibly Aeschylus, but which of Lope's contemporaries would offer parallels?

[23] Presumably Aristophanes. Did Lope have in mind also Vélez de Guevara? Rudolph Schevill [*The Dramatic Works of Luis Vélez de Guevara* (Berkeley, 1937)], commenting on the latter's *comedias de ruido,* says (p. xx): "They must have made exceptional demands on the mechanical and physical capacity of any stage of those days."

palming himself off as a doctor, the better thereby to further the love affairs of Felipe Centellas and the heroine, Lucrecia. The lovers, in the guise of the *pastores*, Olimpo and Belisarda, are acting out Lope's *Arcadia*. Pinzón, the *gracioso*, makes it a play of *apariencias:* not only does he show them a magic cave wherein there are *apariencias* (III, iii, 453-454) — "porque *apariencias* no falten," he says — but the stage directions for the next to the last scene read (III, xii, 459): "Baja don Felipe en una nube y quédese abajo, y al mismo tiempo arrebata otra a Carlos, y vuela arriba." Thus Tirso, in broadest burlesque of the *tramoyistas'* methods, airily wafts his protagonist on the stage — and just as summarily removes the *rival*.

The scene in question is, nevertheless, directly based on one found in Lope's novel[24] which reads as follows: "[Anfriso] fue oído de un hombre rústico, que de aquellas soledades era dueño y desde sus tiernos años, estudi- ando el arte mágica, las habitaba . . . [era] Dardanio, que así se llamaba el mágico." He tells Anfriso: ". . . yo soy aquel gran médico, Dardanio, famoso y conocido en todo aquello que el sol alumbra, temido y respetado en lo que nunca he visto; porque yo tengo fuerza sobre los elementos, tem- plando el fuego, sujetando el aire, humillando la mar y allanando la tierra. *Hago domésticas a mi voz las más rebeldes víboras y sierpas destas horribles cuevas . . .*" In the role of necromancer, Dardanio then conjures up for Anfriso, as examples to incite him, a long series of heroes beginning with the names of Romulus and Remus, passing through those of the Cid and don Alonso de Guzmán el Bueno,[25] and ending with that of "el gran Gonzalo Fernández."

The stage directions of Tirso's plays are as follows (III, iii):

Tocan trompetas, chirimías y toda la música; cáese abajo todo el lienzo del teatro y quede un jardín, lleno de flores y yedra. A la mano derecha esté un purgatorio y en él penando algunas almas. *Y a la iz- quierda un infierno y en él colgado, uno y otro en una tramoya . . . una sierpe y un león a sus lados;* arriba, en medio de esto en otra parte, una gloria y en ella Apolo, sentado en un trono con una corona de laurel en la mano.

Asked for an explanation of this scene, Pinzón — with his background of a two years' stay in Salamanca, followed by military service in Italy — gives the following (III, iii, 453):

---

[24] *BAE,* XXXVIII, 84.

[25] Of don Alonso Pérez de Guzmán, Dardanio says (*ed. cit.,* 85): "Este es aquel valiente caballero, señor de la casa de Toral y cabeza de los Guzmanes, don Alonso Pérez, que mereció ser llamado el Bueno, título que tan pocos han merecido en el mundo, y que también dió España al que ves a su lado, *que es el ilustrísimo don Este- ban Illán,* de tan notorias hazañas . . . . Thus the name of don Alonso de Guzmán el Bueno is even here linked by association with that of don Illán de Toledo, who had dealt in magic.

Ruiz de Alarcón's *La prueba de las promesas* is concerned with don Illán. It is dated by Agustín Millares Carlo [*Obras completas de Juan Ruiz de Alarcón* (Mexico, 1959) II, 749] "hacia 1618." I suspect it to be later.

> El pastor, Criselio —
> que, aunque pastor nigromante,
> consoló en su cueva a Anfriso
> cuando lloraba pesares
> en figura de romero
> (según cuenta en sus anales
> la Arcadia, tercero libro,
> folio ciento y cuatro) — os hace
> ostentación de su ciencia.

Having called the roster of military heroes — one that follows in abbreviated form the list which Lope had given — he concludes by saying:

> Este, pues, a instancia mía
> hoy os quiere hacer alarde
> de sus mágicos secretos . . . .

Asked concerning the scene which has opened up before their eyes, Pinzon explains (p. 454):

> Este es Parnaso de Apolo,
> y todos los circunstantes
> son poetas . . . .
> El Parnaso se compone
> de tres senos o lugares:
> gloria, infierno, y purgatorio
> . . . .
> los de la mano derecha,
> porque mejor se declare,
> en letras góticas dicen:
> Parnaso crítico.

There follows, then, the brief description of those in purgatory, which has been outlined above. Pinzón, thereupon, turns to those in the Inferno, and we have the following conversation — for our purpose on this occasion the important part:

> Felipe: Y ¿quién son los del Infierno?
> Pinzón: Leed esas letras grandes.
> Felipe: Parnaso cómico dicen.
> Lucrecia: Y éstos, ¿no pueden salvarse?
> Pinzón: No han de ir al cielo de Apolo.
> Lucrecia: ¿Por qué culpa?
> Pinzón: Detestables.
>   ¿No es hacer moneda falsa
>   crimen lesee majestatis?
> Lucrecia: Claro está.
> Pinzón: Pues éstos venden
>   a todo representante
>   comedias falsas; con liga
>   de infinitos badulaques
>   han adulterado a Apolo
>   con tramoyas, maderajes
>   y bofetones, que es Dios,

y osan bofetearle,
y están corridas las musas,
que las hacen *ganapanes*,
cargadas de *tantas vigas*,
peñas, fuentes, torres, naves,
que las tienen deslomadas,
y así las mandan que pasen
penas y cargas eternas
a sus culpas semejantes,
y las atormenten *sierpes,*
arpías, grifos, salvajes,
que son los que en sus comedias
introducen ignorantes,
dando al ingenio de palo.

and Lucrecia adds:

Quien tal hace que tal pague.[26]

Having paid his respects to two other comic poets[27] who are likewise in
Hell — with their identity we shall have to be concerned on another occasion
— Tirso then enthrones Lope. Alejandra asks:

¿Quién es aquél que en la silla
tan autorizado y grave
tiene en la mano el laurel,
borla del Petrarca y Dante?

Pinzón: Esa es la gloria de Apolo
y aquél el dios que las llaves
tiene del entendimiento,
y premiar al docto sabe;
la corona es para quien,
escribiendo dulce y fácil,
sin hacerle carpintero,
hundirle ni entramoyarle,
entretiene al auditorio
dos horas, *sin que le gaste*
más de un billete, dos cintas,
un vaso de agua o un guante,
ése se coronorá.

Alejandra: ¿Y los demás?

Pinzón: Que se abrasen,
pues, dándonos pan de palo,
los ingenios matan de hambre.
Los que quisieran saber
los misterios importantes

---

[26] The last words that a criminal sentenced to death would hear. Rodrigo Calderón,
who died on the scaffold as a result of the policy of "strict justice" which Olivares
had initiated, listened to them on October 21, 1621. The *pregón* is given in full by
Andrés de Almansa y Mendoza, *Cartas*, (Madrid, 1886), 99. It ends: "[El Rey] le
manda degollar, para que sea a él castigo y a otros ejemplo: quien tal hace que tal
pague."

[27] One is a "poeta vergonzante que pide trazas de noche de limosna;" the other
is a "poeta de encaje," who puts in his plays "cuatro pasos de las viejas redondillas y
romances . . ."

> *que el sabio Criselio enseña*
> *a los pastores amantes,*
> *a su cueva los convida.*
> *Lucrecia:* Entremos todos a hablarle.
> *Carlos:* Satírico es el doctor.
> *Angela:* Y sus burlas agradables.

In glorifying Lope over Góngora as a lyric poet, at the same time that he exalts him over those dramatists who are writing plays of spectacle that call for much stage machinery, Tirso is asking for a *comedia* that calls for simple stage properties, one that has easy musical verse. In other words, he is holding up the Lopean formula for the *capa y espada* play, which — with its sweet verses and its delicate metaphors — made its primary appeal to the *ear;* and he is decrying the popularity of the *comedia de ruido* which depended on stage effects and called for all kinds of elaborate machinery. In his denunciation, he picks up Lope's metaphor of the stage carpenters, and elaborates it: the muses, loaded down as they are with "beams, boulders, fountains, and towers," have become mere "errand boys" whose backs are being broken under their load. The ignorant poets who are bringing on the stage serpents, harpies, griffins, and savages, belong in Hell, there to be guarded by the very monsters they have introduced into their plays.

The *tramoya* was far from new when *La fingida Arcadia* was written in 1622,[28] but it assumed new importance at court with the accession of Philip IV and the rise to power of Olivares.[29] Luis Vélez de Guevara, known to his contemporaries as *Lauro,* had for many years been writing plays that called for elaborate stage machinery — *comedias de ruido,* they were ordinarily termed. When Rojas, around 1603, in his *Viaje entretenido,* speaks of "farsas de guerra" (and precisely in connection with *tramoyas* or *apariencias*), he probably had in mind such a play as Vélez de Guevara's *El capitán prodigioso y príncipe de Transilvania,*[30] as did Cervantes in 1615 when, in the introduction to his volume of *comedias* and *entremeses,* he spoke of "el rumbo, el tropel, el boato, la grandeza" de las comedias de Luis Vélez de

[28] See, for date, "On the Date of Five Plays by Tirso," *HR,* X (1942), specifically, 191-197. Also below, p.
[29] On this point, see H. Merimée, *Spectacles et comédiens a Valencia (1580-1630),* 186-189. He says, in connection with "le spectacle de la Olivera": "En fait, les premières mentions que j'en ai relevées datent de quelques années plus tard" [than 1618]. Le 19 juillet 1621, la représentation habituelle ne put avoir lieu, parce qu'elle aurait empêché de dresser certaines machines pour la représentation du lendemain. Le 20 août de la même année, on fit à nouveau relâche dans les mêmes conditions: il s'agissait de préparer une "invention" inédite. La mode des mises on scènes compliquées se maintint et prospéra: on soigna les décors, on perfectionna la machinerie . . . etc. . . . *après le plaisir des yeux, le plaisir des oreilles."*
[30] Attributed both to Vélez de Guevara and to Lope de Vega. On this point, see Morley and Bruerton, *The Chronology of Lope de Vega's "comedias,"* 331, and Rudolph Schevill, *The Dramatic Works of Luis Vélez de Guevara,* 368-372. The former study declares, "We do not believe that Lope wrote the play"; the latter: ". . . this drama, both by its content and by its language and its verse, is very characteristic of the muse of Luis Vélez."

Guevara." Lope almost certainly wrote the passage in which San Ginés describes the stage of one dramatist as "un escritorio / con diversas navetas y cortinas; no hay tabla de ajedrez como su lienzo," with the Andalusian school in mind — and even very possibly, Luis Vélez de Guevara. Suárez de Figueroa, in his *Pasajero* of 1617, satirizing plays of *tramoya*, mentions specifically Vélez's play on the Prince of Transylvania.[31] In 1620, Salas Barbadillo, in his *La sabia Flora Malsabidilla*,[32] laughs at a play whose stage decorations included *"naves, galeras, casas de placer, selvas, elefantes, hidras . . . panteras y selvajes."* Here the satire is general in form, but in *Don Diego de Noche*, which was written before July 7, 1621, he has included an *Epistolaria jocoso* wherein he sends *pésames*[33] to a "poeta cómico de que le silbaran una comedia." This *comedia* was — Salas makes evident — one of the *tramoyas* which included in the last act an *apariencia de ángeles* and a horse which unexpectedly bolted. The *"poeta cómico"* who wrote the play was none other than Vélez de Guevara, and it was acted by Roque de Figueroa, a fact which becomes clear, however, only when we study Salas' comments in connection with a satirical poem written by don Antonio de Mendoza. The poem is headed:[34] "Habiendo silbado una comedia de Luis Vélez, dijo Don Antonio de Mendoza: 'Entre los sueltos caballos / de la mosquetera gente / que por el patio silbaron / entre lo Roque lo Vélez . . . .' "

Tirso's satire of the *tramoyistas* in *La fingida Arcadia* is likewise *apparently* general, but in reality it is *very, very* specific. It, too, is directed against Luis Vélez de Guevera and a play (one involving *tramoyas*) which the Andalusian dramatist necessarily wrote shortly before Tirso penned *La fingida*

[31] Suárez de Figueroa [*El pasajero*, (Madrid, 1914) 124], says: "En las de cuerpo [i.e., las comedias de ruido] que (sin las de Reyes de Hungría o Príncipes de Transilvania), suelen ser de vidas de santos. . . ."

[32] Princeps: Madrid, 1621, with an *aprobación* and *licencia* del Ordinario dated October 31, 1620. The *tasa* is February 8, 1621.

[33] Princeps: Madrid, 1623. The *"comisión del ordinario"* is dated July 7, 1621; the *tasa*, November 7, 1623. The *epistolario jocoso* begins fol. 29 v.

[34] Quoted from E. Cotarelo y Mori, *El conde de Villamediana* (Madrid, 1886), 116. It might possibly be argued that Salas Barbadillo's reference is to a play by Andrés de Claramonte, one in which a bolting horse led to the miscarriage of the actress, Ana Muñoz. [See Fernández-Guerra, *Don Juan Ruiz de Alarcón y Mendoza* (Madrid, 1871), 186.] But Ana Muñoz was in 1593 the wife of Antonio de Villegas, who died May 29, 1613. It is hardly probable that in 1621 Salas should have been alluding to an event which had occurred years before.

Arcadia.[35]   The *comedia* in question was entitled *Más pesa el rey que la sangre y blasón de los Guzmanes*.[36]   Let us prove the assertion.

Tirso, you will remember, begins his condemnation of the *tramoyistas* by asserting that they will never reach Apollo's heaven: they are traitors, guilty of "crimen lesee majestatis" in that they are counterfeiting money (*moneda falsa*) by selling to the autores "comedias falsas;" they have, complains the dramatist, adulterated (i.e., cheapened) Apollo with the alloy of "infinitos badulaques," such as *tramoyas, maderajes, bofetones*. Tirso's metaphor, then, compares the traitors to Apollo with those of the realm who were "adulterating" the money, a clear allusion to the *moneda de vellón*,[37] i.e., money of silver adulterated with copper, and to the chief proponent of this policy, the Conde-Duque de Olivares, who was tampering with the coinage in an attempt to make money with which to finance the Thirty Years' War. Elsewhere in this play (I, iv, 438v.), Tirso calls it specifically "moneda vil de vellón."

The stage directions for this scene, it should be remembered, called for *tramoya* on the side that was Hell, one on which were hung a *serpent* and a *lion*. Innocent though their presence may seem — they are apparently nothing but a bit of stage scenery which satirizes the menagerie of animals which the *tramoyistas* were bringing on the stage — they, in reality, point specifically

[35] This play, so evidently written to glorify the Guzmán family, should by all logic have been done not long after Olivares became favorite to Philip IV on March 31, 1621. There is internal evidence that points to that same time. The play contains *silvas* of the first class (some 3.7%), a fact that in and of itself probably points to 1620 or later.

Aside from this, there is an allusion to the fight that Lope was waging against the triumvirate of classicists (Suárez de Figueroa, Torres Rámila, and Mártir Rizo) which began in 1617 and ended in 1623. Lope had satirized Suárez de Figueroa as "perro" and "abubilla"; Torres Rámila as "sastre," "culebra," and [in the Filomela] as "tordo"; Mártir Rizo as "gato". [See Entrambasaguas, *op. cit.*, II (Madrid, 1947), 325-406; in particular, 404.] In the second *sátira*, quoted by Entrambasaguas, he promises in the concluding lines a third *sátira*: "Allí te diré yo del triunvirato / con que encubáis la fama de los buenos / juntándose *culebra, perro y gato*." The whole first *sátira* is given over to the theme of Tórres Rámila as son of a Moorish *sastre* (it ends "Sastre fuiste y serás eternamente.").

These *sátiras* led in 1622 to investigations that began March 24th of that year and ended in early 1623: Torres Rámila was asking for a vacancy in the Colegio Mayor de Ildefonso, one calling for limpieza de *sangre*. Vélez, in *Más pesa el rey que la sangre* (III, 106a), put into the mouth of his *gracioso*, Costanila, the following neat reference to Lope's "triumvirate," and to Torres Rámila's supposed Moorish blood: "El *perrito* / que agora del foso sale / *gateando*, vive Dios / que le he conocido *sastre* / en Marruecos . . ." Yet he hypocritically swore to Pérez Roy on November 11, 1622, when the latter was making his investigations concerning the charge of Moorish blood which Lope had brought in his *sátiras* against Torres Rámila, (*op. cit.*, 118): ". . . en cuanto a las sátiras, oio una vez leer una sátira, digo decir i referir a otro algunos fragmentos." He virtuosly concludes his testimony saying: "no solamente [no] se debe dar crédito, ni puede dar, pero siente que aun peca mortalmente contra justicia el que tal hace." Vélez's play was written in all likelihood in the early months of 1622.

[36] Princeps: First printed as a *suelta* in the seventeenth century. See *BAE*, XLV.

[37] There are unfavorable allusions to *vellón* in some 10 other works of Tirso, written in these same years. These references are important for Tirso's chronology, as I expect to show soon in a study that was begun many years ago.

to the Guzmán coat of arms, and even more specifically to the recent play of *tramoyas* by Vélez de Guevara, *Más pesa el rey que la sangre,* which had made use of the Guzmán scutcheon in glorifying the feats of that noble family. And the scintillating light of that family at the moment was the Conde-Duque de Olivares, who, on becoming *privado* to Philip IV, had trampled ruthlessly under foot all those who had stood close to Philip III.

The origin of the lion and the serpent on the Guzmán coat-of-arms is made clear in a ballad which Durán included in his collection, one he took from a *Códice de la Biblioteca de Salazar, Genealogía de la casa de Guzmán.*[38] Its heading is "De como, estando Guzmán el Bueno a servicio del rey de Marruecos, mató una sierpe y domó un león que con ella combatía." Vélez, in his comedia, *Más pesa el rey que la sangre y blasón de los Guzmanes,* had developed this episode at great length (II, 102-104). The lion, already tamed when the curtain goes up, follows Alonso de Guzmán wherever he may go, on the stage and off it; and the winged serpent, "a terrible monster" that Vélez evidently took delight in painting, perishes in the second act at the hand of Guzmán el Bueno. The stage directions for this scene are: "Don Alonso, armado con peto, espaldar y espada, y una rodela de acero a las espaldas, y el león . . . ." Later ones are: "Sale don Alonso, con la rodela y espada llena de sangre, y Costanilla [i.e., the *gracioso*] con la cabeza de la sierpe." It was a *winged* serpent, that is, a dragon, Vélez tells us — one that would necessarily tend to link the Guzmán victory with that of St. George over the dragon.

Rudolph Schevill,[39] in analyzing this episode of Vélez's play, points to the dramatist's very evident familiarity with many incidents in the life of the hero, some of which he has slightly altered; then he suggests that Vélez must have utilized some history of the house of the dukes of Medina-Sidonia. The guess that Vélez had primary sources for his play is an accurate one, for almost certainly Vélez wrote this work at the behest of the Conde-Duque de Olivares (one branch of Medina-Sidonia's tree), who would naturally have put at the poet's disposal all available materials from the family archives, including the original patent of nobility from Sancho IV wherein are listed the *mercedes* that monarch had given the family. Nor does it require much stretching of the imagination to assume that it was played before an audience which included young Philip IV — all to the end that he be reminded of his great debt to the Guzmanes. The concluding scene of Vélez's play carries these significant lines, spoken by King Sancho IV after Guzman's sacrifice of his son in defense of *Tarifa:*

> que sois el mayor, confieso,
> que a rey ha besado mano
> y éste ha sido el mayor hecho

[38] Quoted from Spencer and Schevill, *The Dramatic Works of Vélez de Guevara,* 192.

[39] *Op. cit.,* 188-193. See in particular, 191-192.

que ha celebrado la historia
de romanos y de griegos;
y, *cumpliendo con algunas*
de las finezas que os debo
estas mercedes os hago
y diga en el privilegio:
"Por cuanto vos, Don Alonso
Pérez de Guzmán el Bueno,
imitasteis a Abrahán
con más invencible esfuerzo,
él, en el dicho no más,
y vos, en el dicho y hecho,
de una vez sacrifica[n]do
a Dios y a mí el hijo vuestro,
de *Niebla* os hago señor
de *Sanlúcar* y *del Puerto*
de Santa María, Palos,
Huelva, Sidonia y *Trigueros;*
y a la gran doña María
Coronel le doy sin esto
a *Olivares* y al *Algaba*
para chapines.

These lines, and the man who penned them, i.e., Luis Vélez de Guevara, must have been a powerful irritant to Tirso, who looked with a jaundiced eye on the new *privado*, not only because of his cheapening of the coin[40] of the realm, but also because he had been the recipient of so many *mercedes* from his sixteen-year-old king. Over and over and over in his works of these years — beginning in 1621 — he has protested the debased coinage,[41] and on no less than three occasions, as I have had occasion to show in a previous study,[42] he had protested the many *mercedes* that Olivares was receiving; in the *Cigarrales* (ed. cit., II, 93), in *Privar contra su gusto* (II, xxv, 357c), and in *La prudencia en la mujer* (III, i, 300b).

But, unless I am greatly mistaken, Tirso has, in this same scene of *La fingida Arcadia*, linked Olivares with another accusation that was being cir-

---

[40] Marañon (*op. cit.*, 314-315) treats Olivares' role in connection with the issues of *vellón* under the heading "El desastre financiero." He says: ". . . las grandes maniobras de este género [i.e., de vellón] se hicieron bajo el reinado de Felipe IV, y por tanto, bajo la máxima responsabilidad de Olivares. En los primeros cinco años de su reinado, lanzáronse emisiones enormes de vellón cuyo valor estuvo, en adelante, sometido a las oscilaciones más bruscas y descabelladas."

[41] The first allusion that I have noted in Tirso's works is in his short novel *Los tres maridos burlados* [ed. Espasa-Calpe, (Madrid, 1942), 216]. It must have been written between April, 1621 and October 8, 1621. When the wife asks the *cajero* if he is indisposed, the latter answers: ". . . si no es el enfado de haber contado hoy más de seis mil reales en *vellón*, no me he sentido más bueno en mi vida." See also my study, "Notes on two Interrelated Plays of Tirso," *HR*, XXVIII (1960), 198, n. 20.

[42] See my study on *La prudencia*, 1144-47. Tirso's chief complaint here was, however, the injustice Philip was showing his father's advisers.

By November 21, 1621, Olivares had recognized the resentment that the *mercedes* were causing and had recommended to the King that he give him fewer of them, saying "Véome a mí más obligado al real servicio de V. M. que otro ningún vasallo . . ."

culated in the capital in the summer and fall of 1622, one which was greatly
perturbing officialdom and one which Marañon has dealt with in his chapter
entitled "Las hechicerías de Olivares."[43] The Conde-Duque was a believer
in witchcraft, as his modern biographer readily concedes: ". . . creía . . . en
algunos disparates que su situación y cultura le debía impedir aceptar."
Around September of 1622 such complaints, which had evidently been floating around for some time before, actually reached the President of the Royal
council, don Francisco Contreras (*op. cit.*, 187): specifically, they involved
one Leonorilla, who was urging certain filters on her customers with the
argument that they were "los mismos que el conde de Olivares daba al rey
conservar su privanza." Thus the favorite was trafficking in witchcraft, and
others actually accused him of possessing powers of black magic. The whole
situation must have been known to Tirso in the summer of 1622 when he
was writing this scene of *La fingida Arcadia.*

The *Parnaso de Apolo,* it is to be remembered, takes place at the entrance
of a cave; and caves were, by long tradition, the abode of necromancers. Lope
and Tirso were acquainted with that tradition, and so was the anonymous
author of the malignant *Cueva de Meliso,*[44] who, at Olivares' fall from
power, brought forth all the wild rumors that he had been collecting against
this favorite in the more than twenty years that the latter had ruled Spain.
In the very first note of the 72 which accompany the text of *La cueva de
Meliso* — each accusation is annotated by the author — he comments on the
evils of the time, adding (p. 552): ". . . no es la menor consultar al demonio
para pedirle avisos . . . ." Having pointed to the Marques de Villena as
an offender in this direction and also to the tradition which associated the
cave of Toledo with black magic, he brings in the name of Meliso, of whom
Diógenes Laercio and Apolidoro had written; one who, he says satirically,
gave admirable precepts of government. In the poem itself, don Gaspar de
Olivares, i.e., Philip IV's *privado,* finds himself separated from his com-
panions on a hunting trip in the Sierra Morena mountains and makes it an
opportunity to enter the cave of Meliso, as Anfriso had entered Dardanio's
in Lope's novel.[45] There Olivares' future is forecast, and there he receives
from the wizard — whom he hails as "gran maestro, de toda ciencia mágica

---

In his will, he gives a complete list of his titles: "Conde de Olivares, Duque de San-
lúcar la Mayor, Duque de Medina de las Torres, Marqués de Eliche, Adelantado Mayor
de la muy noble y muy leal provincia de Guipúzcoa, Gran Canciller de las Indias,
Comendador Mayor de Alcántara, Comendador de Víboras y Segura de la Sierra y de
Herrera, Sumiller de Corps, Camarero y Caballerizo Mayor de S. M. el Rey, de su
Consejo de Estado y Guerra, Alcalde perpetuo de los Alcázares Reales de la ciudad de
Sevilla, de la Casa Real del Buen Retiro y de la de Vaciamadrid y la Zarzuela, Capitán
general de la Caballeria de España y Sevilla y su reino." One can hardly blame his
contemporaries for not taking seriously his protestations concerning the *mercedes* he
was being given. See Marañon, *op. cit.*, 96, n. 3.
[43] *Op. cit.*, 185-190.
[44] Included in *BAE*, LXXIX, 543-557.
[45] See above.

el más diestro que vieran las edades, oráculo mayor de las verdades" — the
following promise, made supposedly in the dawn[46] of the favorite's rise to
power (p. 544):

> que entre héroes has de ser el más perfeto,
> que el mundo ha conocido,
> y poner los antiguos en olvido,
> manifestando el modo
> de governarlo y mejorarlo todo,
> y hacer, con nuevas leyes,
> reyes-privados y privados-reyes.[47]

The magician then recommends to him, one by one, all the Machiavellian
acts with which Olivares was supposed to have brought Spain on evil days.
He begins with the poison which the Count-Duke's father was reputed to
have given to Sixtus V in August, 1616,[48] then passes to the filters which the
privado had used in 1622 in an effort to make secure his power over the
King, and ends with the supposed assassination of don Miguel de Cárdenas,
the Alcalde of the court, who had first taken to the Royal Council the information about Leonorcilla's powders and thereby linked Olivares' name
officially with the use of black magic.

The very name which Tirso has given his necromancer must have some
significance.   Lope had called his wizard in the *Arcadia* "Dardanio," but
Tirso, while retaining the other names of the original, has changed this one
to Criselio.   Now Criselio is the Italianate form of Klesl,[49] who had been
the *privado* of Matías, Emperor of the Holy Roman Empire, until the latter's
death in 1619.   In that position the *privado* had urged on his sovereign a

[46] Olivares says (p. 544a): "Si éste es Meliso, si de él guardo / el más cumplido
aviso a mi privanza / para reinar en ella sin mudanza . . ."

[47] Marañon (*El conde-duque de Olivares*, 99, 100) has written: "Y Olivares sentía
desde lo más hondo de su organismo, como uno de sus impulsos más eficaces, el afán
del mando por el mando mismo . . ." Commenting further on this love of power, he
says: "Subir a los hombres de la nada es lo que más acerca a un hobre a la condición
de Rey, *meta-subconciente del Conde-Duque*." Later he discusses his *emulación real*:
the desire to "govern everything . . ., [de] hacer, con nuevas leyes, reyes-privados y
privados-reyes," was early recognized, as was the "paralytic will" of Philip IV. In-
evitable then was the fight between Olivares and the grandees of the realm.   See
Marañón, *op. cit.*, 87-95.

In a dialogue between Ribato y Pascual, one that is attributed to Villamediana, we
read (ed. Cotarelo, *Conde de Villamendiana*, 199): "Y si al fin los santos lugares /
nunca trocaran los dos / *no queriendo el Rey ser Dios,* / *ni los ministros ser reyes . . .*"

[48] Tirso promised in the closing lines of *La elección por la virtud* a "segunda comedia," which normally would have dealt with *Sixto Quinto's* death.   He apparently
wrote it, for in H. Merimée's *Spectacles et comédiens a Valencia* (p. 173) are listed,
among the plays Juan Acacio had in his possession on March 13, 1627, two entitled:
"Sixto 5º" and "2ᵈ parte de Sixto 5º."   (They follow in the list Tirso de Molina's
Martín Peláez [i.e., *El cobarde más valiente*].   By the very nature of the theme, it
could hardly have failed to be a dangerous one which would certainly have done
nothing to improve relations between the Conde-Duque and Tirso.

[49] See this form of *Klesl* in Morel Fatio's edition of "La guerra del Palatinado,
1620-1621," included in *L'Espagne au XVIᵉ et au XVIIᵉ siècle* (Madrid, 1878), 331-
332; also my study, "Two Interrelated Plays of Tirso." *HR*, XXVIII (1960), 206-207.
Klesl was in the spotlight from January, 1622, to October 23, 1622, and even until
June, 1623, when the Pope managed to free him completely.

policy of peace between Catholics and Protestants. This tolerance, and the man urging it, were so unpopular in certain directions that in 1618 Maximilian had had him imprisoned in a castle in the Tyrol with Archduke Leopold as his jailer. When in 1621 Gregory XV became Pope, he was indignant at this treatment of one wearing the purple (for Klesl was a cardinal of the Church), and as early as January of 1622, he began his efforts to free the prisoner and to bring him to Rome. The attempt, not entirely successful until June, 1623, was opposed by the Archduke Leopold and also by the governor of Milán, who was no other than the Duque de Feria. Just what was Olivares' attitude in this particular matter of Klesl and just what Tirso had in mind on giving the name Criselio to his wizard,[50] I have not been able to discover, but the *Cueva de Meliso* lists the death of the Duque de Feria among those supposed "muertes de grandes que se acumularon al Conde-Duque" (p. 557a).

Such tension, assuming that it existed as early as this, would necessarily have been known to don Jerónimo Pimentel, Captain-general of the Cavalry under Feria; and this is the Pimentel whom Tirso has glorified in *La fingida Arcadia* through the mouth of don Felipe Centellas.[51] The latter tells his beloved Lucrecia (I, iv, 438):

> Dióme el gran duque de Feria,
> milanés gobernador,
> una tropa de caballos
> debajo la protección
> de aquel Pimentel invicto,
> valeroso sucesor
> de aquel padre de la patria,
> de aquel Numa, aquel Catón . . . etc.

There follows extended praise of the father, i.e., the 8th Conde-Duque de Benavente, who had recently died, and of his son, don Jerónimo, both of whom in Tirso's opinion had rendered such distinguished service to the father-land. Again, in the final scene of *La fingida Arcadia*, Tirso glorifies don Jerónimo, this time with Carlos as mouth-piece. What is more; in praising him, he probably mimics the last half of Vélez's title, *Más pesa el rey que la sangre y blasón de los Guzmanes* (III, xiii, 459b):

---

[50] I do not believe there could fail to be a reason — in a scene so carefully worked out as is Tirso's — for his changing the name of Dardanio to Criselio. If Klesl was being accused by his Spanish enemies of witchcraft, I have not been able to find mention of it. Certainly, Francisco de Ibarra, author of *La guerra del palatinado* (see note 49 above) complains of "la ambición y avaricia del cardenal Criselio" (p. 332).

[51] Young Centellas evidently incurred criticism for his lack of responsibility in his conduct of the war. See Pinzón's words (II, ix, 446b). One may suspect that Suárez de Figueroa, in dealing with the lack of military discipline of the times (See his *Varias noticias importantes* [159 v. - 174 v.]) had in mind such casual conduct as Felipe Centellas' when he wrote (165 v.): "No sé qué me diga de algunos *capitanes* destos tiempos, *a quien hace el favor empuñar la gineta en verdes años, sin prudencia y ejercicio.*" He has in mind events in the Piemonte, for he says later (168 v.): "durante la guerra de Piemonte."

> Pastores, en nuestra casa
> tenemos el mejor huésped
> que honró en nuestro siglo a Italia:
> *don Jerónimo, famoso*
> *Pimentel, sol en las armas*
> *y blasón de Benavente;*
> me da aviso en esta carta
> que hoy llegará a ser padrino,
> no de Anfriso y Belisarda,
> de Lucrecia y don Felipe
> Centellas, su camarada
> y amigo.

Even though the setting of *La fingida Arcadia* is supposedly in Valenza del Po, Italy, Tirso was apparently welcoming don Jerónimo's arrival in Madrid in the summer of 1622. In fact, this play must have been finished by August 8, 1622, since in the *Noticias de Madrid*[52] we read, under that date, of the assassination of Fernando Pimentel (his brother) and of Jerónimo's rushing to the latter's aid. That the play was performed in the garden on a warm day of late spring or summer — probably in that of one of the Pimentel's — is almost certain, for most, if not all the scenes, are in the open, and there are at least two references which attest to the heat of the moment. Pinzón speaks (III, ii, 452b) of "el calor que el campo abrasa," and earlier, noting that some of the characters are seated on the ground, he, in his capacity as doctor, gives his comic stamp of approval with the comment (II, xv, 449b): "Si fuera en invierno, / disentería amenazaban / las humedades del suelo."[53] Elsewhere, Felipe speaks specifically of spring (III, i, 451b): "La primavera, / a fiestas ocasionada, / la juventud novelera, / esta quinta celebrada, / estas selvas y ribera, / todo se junta al deseo / de ver mi condesa sana."

These allusions coincide with a literary event of May, 1622, which likewise seems to find reflection in *La fingida Arcadia*. Lope, as he presides over Apollo's Parnassus, is so strongly reminiscent of the literary fiesta that celebrated the sanctification of San Isidro — over which he had presided in late May of 1622 and from which he had excluded his enemies, the Gongorists — that it is logical to conclude that Tirso had in mind Lope's role on that occasion and that he began his play shortly thereafter.[54] In that literary event,

[52] *Noticias de Madrid, 1621-27*, edited by Angel González Palencia (Madrid, 1942), 31-32. "Acudieron sus dos hermanos, don Gerónimo y don Vicente, puestas sobre sus camisas sus sotanillas y hallaron muerto a su hermano . . ."
[53] Facetiously he quotes Galen as weighty authority for this opinion. See n. 10 above.
[54] In 1942 I wrote ("On the Date of Five Plays by Tirso," *HR*, X [1942], 197): "For the present, it is safe to say that this play was penned between November 8, 1621 and March 1, 1623, when the decrees against the collars and cuffs were put into effect. In all probability, it was composed in late 1622 or early 1623." I now believe, on the strength of further study, that it was done between the fiestas given in honor of San Isidro's canonization, and the 8th of August of 1622. The "cartel," which was printed for the *Justa poética* that accompanied the fiestas, "se puso en el teatro

interestingly enough, Vélez de Guevara had taken no part. As Lope's satire of the *tramoyistas*, found in *Parte XVI*, was already in print since the preceding December, Vélez may well have felt that Lope was casting stones in his direction.

One may wonder that Tirso should have dared to satirize the all-powerful Conde-Duque in any such fashion, but it is not necessary to go far for the answer. This play was done as a *particular*, and Tirso knew that in penning it for the Pimentels he was writing for an audience that shared his sentiments about Olivares. Members of this family — originally of Portuguese origin — had been all powerful during Philip III's reign, and in many directions. The greatly respected eighth Conde-Duque de Benavente, so highly praised by Tirso in this play,[55] had, through two marriages, left numerous progeny, most of whom were, during that gentle monarch's life, holding high positions either in the royal household, in the church, or in the military. The father himself had been in charge of Italian affairs during the late years of Philip III's reign, and during that monarch's absence in Portugal he had virtually determined Spain's foreign policy: Don Jerónimo's wife, María Eugenia de Bazán y Benavides,[56], fourth Marquesa de Santa Cruz, was maid-of-honor to the Queen in 1622. The new ninth Conde de Benavente (Juan Francisco Pimentel) was *mayordomo mayor* to the Queen, and on October 20, 1622, he married Leonor Pimentel,[57] maid-of-honor to the Infanta María, and sister to don Antonio Pimentel y Toledo (4th Marqués de Távara) who had for wife the Duque de Lerma's niece. This fourth Marqués de Távara had, before Philip IV's accession, even hoped to hold the very position in the King's affections that Olivares now held. Villamediana's *Vita bona* makes clear that this had been his dream — at the same time it makes evident the tension between him and the Conde de Olivares. Two strophes of that *chacona* read as follows:[58]

que para dicha justa se levantó en el segundo patio de palacio el día 26 de mayo."
See Pérez Pastor, *Bibl. madr.*, III, 130.
Tirso had taken part in that *justa poética*.
[55] See I, iv, 438. He is "aquel padre de la patria / . . . aquel Numa, aquel Catón / que fertilizando canas / a la Iglesia dió un pastor, / un mayordomo a su reina, / tres columnas a su Dios, / tres Alejandros a Marte, / a España, hijos veintidós, / mil glorias a su alabanza / y a medio siglo un Héctor."
[56] See García Carraffa, *Enciclopedia heráldica y genealógica*, under the name of *Bazán*.
[57] See *Noticias de Madrid*, 40. The notice reads: "A 20, se casó el Conde de Benavente con mi Señora Doña Leonor Pimentel, Dama de la Señora Infanta y hermana del Marqués de Tábara. Fueron padrinos los señores Infantes." The name was apparently pronounced at times with the accent on the 2nd syllable. I have preferred Távara because their ancestral home was in Távara (Zamora).
[58] See E. Cotarelo y Mori, *El conde de Villamediana*, 259, 262. The two strophes about Távara have by some mischance been separated, but they have to do with the same Távara, I feel sure. I have not been able to identify Varelilla.
The Távara family is included under the Pimentels in García Carraffa's *Enciclopedia heráldica*. This branch was descended from Pedro Pimentel Vígil de Quiñones (the 5th son of Alonso Pimentel de Mayorga and doña María Vígil de Quiñones), who was "señor de la villa de Távara (Zamora). They were linked through marriage with

> Olivares se desvela,
> con profana ostentación,
> por ser en toda occasión
> jefe de la parentela;
> Varelilla se las pela,
> que este señor andaluz
> le dejó entre cara y cruz
> ye el de Tábara blasona . . .
> En su pleito divertido
> de Tábara está el señor;
> él es muy grande hablador
> y con eso algo ha perdido.
> *Revienta por ser valido*
> y que la corte lo crea,
> más el alba que el desea
> no se reirá en su persona.

Thus it is evident that there had been keen rivalry between this fourth Távara, a Pimentel of Valladolid, and the Conde de Olivares. What almost certainly made matters worse was that Olivares was also a Pimentel and that his mother, María Pimentel y Fonseca, was likewise from Valladolid. Still again, Olivares' wife was doña Inés de Zúñiga y Velasco, a fact which made him related through marriage to don Jerónimo (of the main branch of the Pimentels), for the mother of the latter was doña Mencía de Zúñiga y Requesens.[59] This was, then, a family war.

The Pimentels must have realized early that their position under the new regime — with Olivares at the helm — was far from being as secure as it had been in the days of Philip IV's father. Their strength lay now in the favor they held with the Queen, the Infanta María, and the two Infantes, Fernando and Carlos.[60] All were supposedly inimical to Olivares because of his influence over the King.

the Enríques family and the Toledos (of the House of Alba). This fourth Marqués de Távera became "Virrey de Valencia y de Sicilia." He died while holding the latter place in 1627. See *Noticias de Madrid*, 159.

[59] Jerónimo Pimentel was the son of the eighth Conde-duque de Benavente by his second wife, doña Mencía de Zúñiga y Requesons. Thus when Olivares' uncle, don Baltasar de Zúñiga (at one time *ayo* to young Prince Philip) was made minister to the new king in 1621, he represented supposedly a link of peace between these two powerful houses. In reality, don Baltasar had been set up merely as a figure-head by the power-loving Olivares, and when he died on October 6, 1622, it was said that his death was due to poison from his nephew, the Conde-Duque. See Marañón, *op. cit.*, 49.

Don Gerónimo Pimentel, almost certainly through his wife's influence with the Queen, continued to flourish. Around October 15, 1622, we read in Almansa y Mendoza's *Cartas* (p. 148): "a D. Gerónimo Pimentel, general de la caballería de Milán, dieron título y mil ducados de ayuda de costa." And later (p. 155): "a don Jerónimo Pimentel hicieron del Consejo de Guerra." And in the *Noticias de Madrid* we read (p. 119): "a 30 de mayo de 1625 dió el Rey título de Marqués de Bayona a don Gerónimo Pimentel, hijo del Conde de Benavente, General que era de la Caballería del Estado de Milán."

[60] As one reads the various *avisos* having to do with the Pimentels in these years, it would seem as if the Queen, the Princess María, and the two Infantes made special effort to honor members of the Pimentel family. It was to doña Leonor Pimentel, sister of the fourth Távara, that the second half of the *fiestas* of Aranjuez were in

Accordingly, Tirso must have known on penning his satirical scene of *La fingida Arcadia,* that he was writing not only for an audience cognizant of all the gossip against Olivares that was floating about the court in 1622, but also for one which was entirely sympathetic to that gossip. To that audience he was criticizing the new *privado* for: 1) his monetary policy; 2) his glorification of his ancestors and the *mercedes* he was receiving for *their* deeds; and, 3) for his traffic with black magic.

As for Vélez de Guevara, he was, in Tirso's eyes, guilty not only of writing *tramoyas* and thus changing the *comedia* into one of spectacle, but because he was exalting with those *tramoyas* the new pride of the Guzmanes. And if Olivares was, for Vélez, the honor of the Guzmanes, Jerónimo Pimentel was, for Tirso, the glory of the Pimenteles.[61]

May, 1622, entrusted. When in October, 1622, she married the ninth Conde de Bena-vente, *mayor-domo* to the Queen, Prince Carlos and Princess María were their *padrinos* and "his Majesty came from San Lorenzo el Real to be present at the wedding." (See Almansa y Mendoza, *Cartas,* 148). Moreover, when the daughter of María Eugenia de Bazán y Benavides (wife to Jerónimo) was married to her uncle, the Marqués de Xavalquinto, "comió la novia con los Reyes en público, que fue de ver, en asiento aparte desviado de el de la Reina nuestra Senora, cosa de una vara . . . y el novio comió con el Conde de Benavente, Mayordomo Mayor de la Reina." See *Noticias de Madrid,* 36.

This ninth Conde de Benavente was having trouble with Olivares as early as June, 1622, (*Noticias de Madrid,* 27) and in the *Casa de los Condes de Benavente* (ms. 11569, B. N., f. 24 v.), it is specifically stated: ". . . murió de sentimiento de verse desfavorecido del Rey cuando la lealtad y amor con que sirvió y el querer excusar algunos lances, *de que dió cuenta al Conde de Olivares,* fué causa de mandarle retirar a su casa sin hacerle merced, ni habérsele pagado los gajes que le quedaron debiendo del tiempo que sirvió para satisfacer sus empeños, que fueron muchos."

He apparently lost his father's title of "Conde-Duque de Benavente" when the father died on November 8, 1621. I have somewhere heard that the title "Conde-Duque de Olivares" — by which Olivares was known (Marañón, *op. cit.,* 95) after he was made "Duque de Sanlúcar la Mayor" in 1626 — was granted him to the end that he could boast of the same title as the eighth Conde-Duque de Benavente. In the *Noticias de Madrid* (p. 32), under date of August 11, 1622, he is already called "Conde-Duque."

[61] In the mind of the reader, there may well be at this point a question: Is there in Tirso's works other satire of Luis Vélez de Guevara which will substantiate my inter-pretation of this scene in *La fingida Arcadia?* The answer is Yes, — but it must be added on another occasion.

I should again like to acknowledge my debt to the University Women, the Univer-sity of Pennsylvania, and the Guggenheim Foundation for aid in difficult times that made it possible for me to carry on my research in European libraries.

SMITH COLLEGE STUDIES IN HISTORY

Volumes Published

* Starred items are out of print.